My Epic Ride of 2020

Criss Crossing the Country During COVID-19

T. DAVID MILLS

outskirts press

Dedication

In writing this book, I could not help but think about the people that either enabled me to write this book or inspired me to ride motorcycles in the first place. On the latter front are two significant people – my father-in-law Al Combs and my good friend Dennis Hoyt. Riding motorcycles has not been a lifelong endeavor for me having started riding around 1994, but my enthusiasm is still extremely high, and I do thoroughly enjoy it. I believe both Al and Dennis have been riding since childhood or at least young adulthood. Al dated my mother-in-law, Janie on a motorcycle and he would always give any of the grandchildren who wanted to take a ride at least a tour around the block. I believe Dennis grew up riding motorcycles along with at least one of his three brothers.

Returning to the former group of encouragers, my wife Roxanna has to rise to the top. While we did not always see eye-to-eye on all fronts, I was able to allay at least most of her fears for me traveling across the country alone on a motorcycle. We discussed it with Dennis, and we all ended up with the agreement that I would not go through any areas that did not appear safe to do so. I would check in, on a daily basis, with Roxanna to be sure that she knew where I really ended up and that I was safely encased in my motel room for each night.

As for my writing the book after the trip, my wife and I had a few discussions about the time commitment and my tendency to "go all in" whenever I take up a project or hobby. We settled into a routine where I would be able to use my laptop during the time we spent in our den viewing TV shows or movies in the evenings. As part of our agreement, I would refrain from jumping onto the computer during every spare minute between activities in which we both were engaged. We navigated through the twists and turns much like motorcycling in the mountains – deliberate actions.

I would be remiss if I did not also give a shout out to my good friends at Street and Trail Motorsports (https://www.streetandtrail.com/) in Evans, Georgia. For many years, before I was playfully called a traitor for riding a Harley-Davidson®, the great people there supported me as I rode Honda, Suzuki, Yamaha, and Kawasaki motorcycles including graciously supporting me riding in many Ride for Kids® events. I am still allowed on the premises with open arms and an occasional hug, for which I am immensely grateful.

Table of Contents

The Concept

The idea of riding a motorcycle on US 50 end-to-end first came to me when I was making my "biker bucket list" and included US 50 in my list of rides to take. I also generated a list of U.S. highways, as part of that bucket list, that I wanted to ride end-to-end, which, of course, included US 50. Why US 50 you may ask? Well, my high school (the original James Wood High School, in Winchester, Virginia) was located on Route 50. Route 50 from Winchester to Washington, D.C. was a well-traveled road many times during high school and college days and later, when I began riding motorcycles, I rode on parts of it.

In 2003, after I had been riding motorcycles for a number of years, I started considering what would become some parts of my biker bucket list. After coming across a site on the internet called US 50 Coast to Coast (http://route50.com/), I made contact with the site's owner and author of the book, "US 50 Coast to Coast", Wulf Berg. I purchased copy number 451 of 500 of the first edition of the limited printing. Wulf and I exchanged emails from that point on and, while we never actually met, I feel we became friends. Wulf is also a Christian and published "My Pilgrimage with God" each week where he shared a spiritual message with Christian believers via email. I lost contact with Wulf, but I still appreciate his previous work putting together his US 50 book. I did; however, recently re-establish contact with Wulf and plan to stop in and visit sometime.

This book was not what was envisioned as the first concept of "A Biker's Bucket List" series, but it needed to be first because it is important to me to get it out as close as possible to the year of my epic experience. Hopefully, there will be others that fill in my vision for a biker's bucket list series of books, but we shall see.

Another reason for putting this book ahead of any other of my potential literary aspirations, is that I made this trip during the COVID-19 pandemic scenario and felt driven to share my story of that aspect of the trip as well. I travelled through twenty-nine states, including some which may have had quarantine restrictions in place, but I just rode on through because I had not been exposed to the virus, was not sick, and was not going to stay anywhere for 14 days, no matter what. No state authorities have tracked me down and arrested me so far and I know I did not bring COVID-19 to any of them!

The return leg of this cross-country journey was on US 20. As stated earlier, I had been planning for many years to take US 50 end-to-end, but I had never really addressed the return trip home. About two years ago, during one of the Combs Clan Rider Group (more on that later) Spring riding retreats, a new friend, Randy Hesler, said he would ride the cross-country trip with me and suggested returning on US 20, the longest US Highway. I took it to heart and starting planning in earnest on US 20 as the return route. We settled on July 2020 as the right time for the trip and the excitement started churning up a lot of ideas and researching of where to stay, where to eat and what to see along the way.

The Planning

Trying to achieve a balance between the overall trip duration, the daily mileage goal, finding destinations with adequate lodging, refueling points based on riding history as well as interesting attractions to visit turned out to be no small task. Two years of earnest planning required countless revisions to the original pen to paper plan, but I tried to stay with the criteria of less than 400 miles per day. Day 1 was the exception, on which I had planned to be alone anyway, was going to be over 500 miles to reach Portsmouth, Virginia that first night. I managed to reach an agreement with my wife on a 26-Day duration based on the logic, that to make a trip of at least 9200 miles, mathematically would take at least 23 days at 400 miles per day, so 26 days seemed to be reasonable to allow for variations and the potential need to have a shorter day or two for a little respite.

The route was already set by the fact that US 50, US 101 and US 20 were the main reasons for the trip, the route from home to US 50 and the route home from US 20 were the variables. I chose to include sections of US Highways, which are on my bucket list to ride end-to-end, for those legs of the journey. These sections were going to be by myself anyway, since the original plan was to meet in Ocean City, Maryland to begin the westward trek on US 50. Choosing US 378, US 17, and US 301 to ride up toward Ocean City, I could then lay out a plan for "attractions" along the way. You know, Harley-Davidson® dealerships and so forth. At any rate, Day 1 was always going to be ride the roads, stop at the dealerships, pick up shirts and poker chips and get to Portsmouth. (Harley-Davidson® dealerships typically have poker chips with their logo or dealership name printed on them that many bikers collect as souvenirs of visits to those dealerships.) The other days had a little more flexibility, so there were a number of "potential" attractions along the way that made the list in the plan.

The research for attractions was based on information I found in a myriad of sources, which are outlined in the list at the back of the book. I did use Google Maps a great deal as I could use it on my computer and synchronize with my phone so all of my saved locations would be on both devices. I do not know how many times I changed those selections, but when I performed a "tracked changes" to my table in Word®, I had to laugh at the amount of red that was on the revised version. No day remained the same as the plan, as all had at least one or more alternative results.

Maintaining the notion of 400 miles or less per day and trying to pick daily destinations which included adequate lodging choices was a little more challenging than one might first believe. Traveling on the US Highways as opposed to Interstates means that all of the commercial benefits along the Interstates may not always be available along the US Highways, which usually run through smaller towns. This situation makes it a little more of a challenge to find locations that have the desired facilities within the distance parameters put in place as part of the decision-making criteria. When you pick one location, it may have an impact on the next location along the chosen highway, which also has a ripple effect on location choices down the line. The planning definitely was an iterative process with multiple changes and alternatives identified before landing on "The Plan". Even then, I still had to make an "audible" (using a football term) more than once to allow for changes encountered along the way, so plans are necessary, but you cannot be put out too much when they have to change. You just have to "go with the flow" as the saying goes.

Locating restaurants followed the same pattern as that put in place for lodging, but with the added burden of locating stops along the way for lunch. You cannot forget about lunch, you know. That part of the equation could sometime be a little more of a challenge because the time of day normally reserved for mealtime did not always align with the location of the traveler at that time. Add to that the limiting effect of the COVID-19 restrictions meant some restaurants may not be open at that time if at all. It was still necessary to at least have a target location close to the normal mealtime. Not having any plan meant you could go hungry for a while to get to locations where there is nourishment, so it became somewhat crucial to know what was and was not available. Even then, situations changed as you will see as the story unfolds.

Riding across the country alone, I wanted to be sure that I had adequate self-defense apparatus (code for firearms) with me and that I would not be in violation of the unconstitutional gun laws imposed by each state on the route. Using several sites, I tried to capture the essence of each of the various state restrictions so that I could know what I had to do when. As it turns out, with very few exceptions, I maintained my control over my various firearms without too much complication.

The Preparation

Traditional Sewing of Do-Rags

For several years I have been sewing do-rags for our Combs Clan Rider Group Spring ride weekends for those of us who could make the ride. I started sewing them while I was working at the V.C. Summer Nuclear Plant construction site and staying near Jenkinsville, South Carolina in my 30-foot camper. It made for an enjoyable pastime, a sense of accomplishment when completed, and provided useable head gear for the riders in the group. The embroidery for this trip was performed on my wife's machine (I have used it more than she has) based on a design I made to show the US Highway shields for US 50 and US 20. I also made masks to be compliant with COVID-19 requirements at the various establishments that might require them.

Previously Implemented Equipment

Back in 2018, I purchased a summer riding jacket from Treasure Coast Harley-Davidson® when I was visiting my sister in Stuart, Florida because I had been looking at them online and not all dealerships carried them. I first saw one and tried it on while on a motorcycle weekend in Townsend, Tennessee as our group rode through Cherokee, North Carolina. I deferred buying one there, thinking I could get one "back home", but none of the local dealerships carried them. By chance, Treasure Coast was having a sale event, so I got a really good deal on the jacket. I really enjoyed having it for the trip as it provided protection as well as a cooling effect through the cool mesh technology design.

Another recommended enhancement I installed on the bike previously is a Chrome Kuryakyn Super Deluxe Wolo® Bad Boy Air Horn Kit, which lets other riders and drivers know you are there when they invade your space. Be careful, though as you might startle someone into a sudden heart attack or other reaction.

The Trunk

To make a cross country trip, I knew I needed a lockable trunk or "Tour-Pak" for my Road King®. I had used my Nelson-Rigg® backpack and roll bag (for my C-PAP machine) on many trips where we stayed in one location and took daily loop rides, so that meant ride to the home base location, unpack, and then ride for a few days, then ride home. Riding to a different location, on a daily basis, meant the bike would be open to long periods of exposure to inquisitive minds, so a lockable trunk would put my mind at ease. It would also make the overnights easier to leave all the clothes packed in the trunk except what was needed for the next day, instead of off-loading and reloading the backpack on the luggage rack.

I must confess, I went with the DIY approach for the trunk and purchased a color-matched Tour-Pak from Nasty Hog. While maybe not the quality of a genuine Harley-Davidson® component, it was significantly less expensive and I rationalized that I was not necessarily going to leave it on the bike after the trip, so if it could make the trip, I would be fine with that. It was made for fit-up with the genuine Harley-Davidson® H-D Detachables system for mounting and it worked really well. I ordered the necessary components and then added a few genuine Harley-Davidson® parts to mate up the lights with my Road King, which was not originally made for a Tour-Pak. I managed to make the connections work and all the lights worked as I had desired. Adding the genuine Harley-Davidson® Tour-Pak liner concealed the wiring and connections underneath. I made connections in there with E-Z Connect Wire Terminal® sets I purchased from Joe Florida, since I had used his stuff on previous bikes.

https://nastyhog.com/collections/tour-packs
https://joeflorida.com/

THE TRUNK BAG

I wanted to have a bag that would hold my C-PAP and all the overnight things like toothbrush, toothpaste, floss, shampoo, body wash, deodorant and so forth as well as some containers for poker chips. For the poker chips, I used several used prescription bottles that the chips fit in perfectly, so space was necessary to accommodate them. For this bag, the genuine Harley-Davidson® Onyx Premium Luggage Tour-Pak Rack Bag was the choice. Big Sky Harley-Davidson® offered the best deal with free shipping, so that was my selection. I was not disappointed as it fit on my rack and had quick-disconnect straps which made it easy for the daily on/off exercise.

https://shopbigskyharley.com/

THE TAIL LIGHTS

To reassure my wife that I would be seen on the road from behind (she is big on my having as much rear lighting as possible), I added a Custom Dynamics Saddlebag Fillerz Tail Lights to add tail, turn, and brake lighting in between the saddlebags and the rear fender. They are simple to install and really light up the rear end.

https://www.customdynamics.com/fillerz-chrome

THE SEAT

For my riding comfort, even though I had planned on riding 400 miles or less each day, I decided an upgrade from the stock Road King seat was in order. A riding friend from Kentucky, Mike Broadus, mentioned on one of our Spring bike ride weekends that he was really pleased with his Ultimate seat on his Kawasaki Vulcan 2000, so I checked into it. They made me a custom seat complete with black-center studs to match the original Road King studs I had, and it turned out great. I bought the two-piece seat with the rider backrest and it really looked nice. The question was, would it do the trick? The only way to answer that was to try it out. So, try it out I did, and it really did provide a comfortable location for my buttocks to settle into for the long haul.

https://ultimateseats.ca/

The Handlebars

With the new riding position due to the seat change, I wanted a little more elevation and pull-back for the hand position, so I looked around for a suitable upgrade.to the stock Road King setup. After a great deal of searching and trial and error, I found a set that worked, which is the KhromeWerks 12" Rise Handlebar for the Road King.

https://www.khromewerks.com/

Non-Functional Chrome

Of course, you do not take a cross country motorcycle trip without assuring that you have as much new chrome as you can afford showing off your bike. That being said, I wanted to dress up Annabelle a little bit, so I added a License Plate Frame, Passing Lamp Visors and Headlamp Visor from Harley-Davidson® and ISO®-Brake Pedal Pad for FL and Longhorn ISO®-Shift Pegs from Kuryakyn. Additional non-functional chrome may be added in future, but that was enough for this trip.

https://www.harley-davidson.com/us/en/index.html
https://www.kuryakyn.com/

The Test Ride

Just having all the parts and pieces does not mean that is all that is needed. I knew I had to load everything up as if I was actually taking the long ride to become accustomed to the change in center of gravity and handling. That being said, I did load everything on the bike and did several loops several different times to make sure I had no surprises when I was really "out there." All went well and Annabelle made the adjustments perfectly. Annabelle and I had no trouble with any of the equipment added and felt ready for the multi-thousand-mile ride across America.

About the Combs Clan Rider Group

The Combs Clan Rider Group was "formed" several years ago when my father-in-law, Al Combs, and several members of his family – son Curt, daughter Dawn, son-in-law David, son-in-law Lance, me, nephew Matt and some non-family interlopers from time to time – started going on ride weekends to various places. The make-up of the group has morphed over the years as some participate and some cannot for various reasons (like maybe, no bike?), but we have sort of loosely tried to have a Spring ride on an annual basis. Matt and I are pretty much the last ones standing so to speak, as most others are not able to make the Spring rides. My father-in-law is 91 years old and now has a CanAm Spyder, but he has to look after my mother-in-law who has health issues and really cannot be left alone much. We all have very fond memories of the times we did have together over the years, whether it was one of our ride weekends or a Ride for Kids® event that we used to attend. One of our members, my brother-in-law Lance, was killed several years ago when he and Al were riding on Main Street in Spartanburg, SC heading toward the nearby Indian manufacturing facility, when a large whitetail buck bolted across the road and collided with him. We all have a "Brother Lance" patch we wear in his honor.

About the Photos

Most of the photos in this book are captured using an old Contour barrel type camera that I call my "dash cam" which is mounted on my handlebar. I have included most of them unretouched straight from the upload from the camera to the computer, so you will notice the reflection of the red body of the camera at times when the sun is behind me. I also chose not to edit out any of the bug splatter or raindrops which I think adds to the true nature of riding a motorcycle in all sorts of conditions.

The selfies were taken with my Samsung Galaxy S7 smartphone and my newly acquired Fugetek FT-569 Portable Aluminum Bluetooth Remote Selfie Stick and Tripod. I had taken it out on my test ride to get acquainted and familiarize myself with the ins and outs of setting it up. I was really pleased with the ease of use all through the trip.

About the Quotes and Footnotes

My original idea of inserting quotes and associated links into the verbiage of the book was altered after some discussion with my wife who was performing a screening of the book for readability and recommended not having them in the main body. She wanted to read more about the ride and not be distracted by historical and location quotes and references and we agreed that many other readers would see it the same way. Not everyone is as interested in learning and sharing about the history as I might be. I only left a very few in the body and created a list in the back of the book indexing the quotes and links that I researched either prior to the ride or after seeing the area and researching after the fact. Hopefully, the history junkies, like me, can refer to the quotes and links as they wish when reading about my travel story.

The Camera I refer to as my "Dash Cam" is rather old and not made anymore but gets the job done

My insulated mug and the saddlebag pouch where I stored my Pedialyte packs for riding in high deserts and mountains

Of course I had to make a fully loaded test ride prior to leaving on the trip and Annabelle performed beautifully

I made several Do-Rags for the trip as well as several masks due to COVID-19

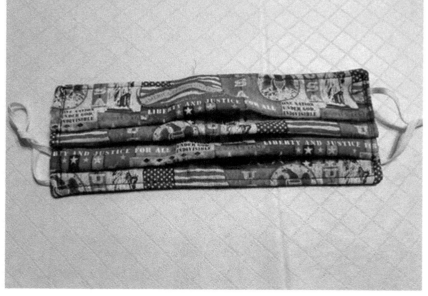

Day 1

Plan

Day	Starting Point / Ending Point	Miles / Ride Time	Potential Lodging	Potential Dining at Destination	Potential Attractions En Route
1 (Thur, Jul 9)	Augusta, GA Portsmouth, VA	547 10:04	Red Roof Inn Norfolk	Five Boroughs Restaurant	• Gas Stop at Little Fisher Truck Stop between Sumter and Conway; • Breakfast at Faye's Diner, Scranton, SC (Take-out); • Harley Shop at the Beach, North Myrtle Beach, SC; • Beach House H-D, Shallotte, NC; • Gas up at Speedway in Wilmington, NC; • Carolina Coast H-D, Wilmington, NC; • Lunch at Ruth's Kitchen, Wilmington, NC (Take-out); • New River H-D, Jacksonville, NC; • H-D of New Bern, New Bern, NC (On Us 70); • Gas up at Shell in New Bern, NC (On US 70); • Bayside H-D, Portsmouth, VA (If before 1900)

Actual

Day	Starting Point / Ending Point	Miles / Ride Time	Lodging	Dining at Destination	Attractions En Route
1 (Thur, Jul 9)	Augusta, GA Portsmouth, VA	547 10:04	Red Roof Inn Norfolk - Portsmouth, VA		• Gas at Pineview Exxon at I-95; • Bojangles near Myrtle Beach on 501 (Dine-In); • Harley Shop at the Beach, North Myrtle Beach, SC; • Beach House H-D, Shallotte, NC; • Gas up at Circle K, Jacksonville, NC; • Carolina Coast H-D, Wilmington, NC; • New River H-D, Jacksonville, NC; • Bayside H-D, Portsmouth, VA (Arrived after 1900, so back in morning)

The first day, after getting rained on near Columbia, South Carolina an hour away from home, then putting rain gear on, then stopping to take it off again, I found myself on US 378 headed East to get to its end point in Conway, South Carolina. Little did I know that starting out on US 378 that I would also see this construction sign which would be a preview of more to come in almost every state through which I was about to travel. The rain was only a minimal threat from that point on as I was in and out of small showers that did not amount to much, so I wasn't concerned about getting wet anymore.

Since I am known as "Papa" to my kids and grandkids, I thought it appropriate to turn the handlebars toward the side to make sure I caught a picture of Papa's General Store in Conway's downtown area, which is near the eastern end of US 378. Conway is a genuinely nice little town, well, actually it is not so little with a population of over 20,000. Established in 1732, originally as Kingston, it was later named Conwayborough, for General Robert Conway, a general in the South Carolina State Militia. The South Carolina General Assembly shortened the town's name to Conway in 1883.

Conway was a river town with the main industry being what they call "naval stores" which is kind of a lumber and turpentine type of industry. It depended largely on the Waccamaw River, which flows by the town, for transportation of people and goods. Conway is basically South Carolina's historic River Town. In 1887, the railroad reached the town adding another transportation alternative and the town was incorporated in 1898.

I took US 501 from Conway to reach Myrtle Beach and US 17, the second US highway targeted to complete a significant portion of on this trip. I needed to catch a lot of US 17 from that point North to complete as much of the highway from one end to the other. That, my friends, was supposed to be the first in a series of "One Biker's Bucket List" books to include riding a myriad of US highways from one end to the other, "End to End" so to speak. Since they have not yet developed into reality, and this one was somewhat imperative that I complete in a timely fashion, we start with the middle of the overall story, with the prequel and subsequent volumes (hopefully) to tell the rest of the story. I have ridden a lot of US 17 going South from home. but needed the part headed North from Myrtle Beach to Warrenton, Virginia where I had left off riding home from its northern terminus in Winchester, Virginia.

The first Harley-Davidson® shop stop was the Harley Shop at the Beach in North Myrtle Beach, South Carolina where I met Lori, (who is also from Virginia), and had been working at the Richmond, Virginia Harley Davidson® before going to Myrtle Beach. The Harley Shop at the Beach was the first of forty-one that I was able to visit and obtain photos of me with the bike in front of the shop for the H.O.G.® Ride 365 contest for dealerships visited. [1]

Continuing on US 17, the next one up the line was Beach House Harley-Davidson® in Shallotte, North Carolina, where I met a future friend Cheree at the Motorclothes counter. She was genuinely nice and helped me with my Tee-shirt and poker chips and we had a nice chat. Everybody there was extremely nice. Shallotte is most likely named for the river of the same name that runs through the town.

Pulling out onto US 17, I got behind a box (that is what I am going to refer to all the trucks or big RV's that quite often manage to get in front of me] on US 17 as I was continuing North. It does not matter what kind of highway it is, but they look like a big square box, so I just called them boxes. There is a photo montage of all the boxes I got behind in the back of this book.

Farther up the coast there was Carolina Coast Harley-Davidson® in Wilmington, North Carolina. I met some nice folks in there, picked out my poker chips and then continued on through some of the showers from the scattered clouds. It was an in and out of showers type of day all along the Atlantic coast.

Heading up towards Jacksonville, North Carolina staying on US 17 I stopped at New River Harley-Davidson® in Jacksonville, and met Carlene and Rikka, who both worked there. Carlene helped me with picking out my poker chips and Rikka was going to put my Ride for Kids® information on the Facebook page for New River Harley-Davidson®. They are extremely nice ladies, and Rikka and I talked for a long time about the perils of getting wet without rain gear while wearing waterproof boots. Wetness soaks through jeans into socks, if you wear high socks as I do, which then soaks into the interior of the waterproof boots. It took a day and a half for my boots to dry out after two nights of airing out in front of the air conditioner vent.

After visiting New River Harley-Davidson®, I then headed up towards New Bern, North Carolina staying on US 17 and bypassed New Bern because of time constraints – I was trying to get to Bayside Harley-Davidson® up in Portsmouth, Virginia before they closed thinking that they would be staying open till 8:00 o'clock as it was indicated on the website. It turns out they were only open till 7:00 and I got there around 7:30.

Some tar snakes were out and about on one stretch of US 17. They can really make for a treacherous journey in the right (or maybe I should say wrong) conditions. For non-riders, "tar snakes" are the squiggly tar sealant repairs of the cracks that eventually appear in asphalt surfaces. When wet or when extremely hot, they can do squirmy things with motorcycle tires, so we try to be aware and avoid them when possible. At least, that is the goal.

I also noticed along the way that they are really proud of Beaufort County in North Carolina, judging by the sign on US 17, and maybe rightfully so as it has a long history. [1a]

Riding into the Roanoke River National Wildlife Refuge on US 17 in North Carolina and crossing the Roanoke River bridge was remarkably interesting, once I did a little research after the fact. The Roanoke River Bridge linking Martin and Bertie counties is named for state Trooper Tom Davis, who was killed by bank robbers in Williamston on Sept. 2, 1975. He had stopped a vehicle he saw run a red light at the intersection of U.S. 17 and U.S. 64. He did not know the vehicle contained three suspects who had just robbed a bank in nearby Jamesville. When Trooper Davis leaned down to speak with the driver, he was shot with a sawed-off shotgun. In 2004, the North Carolina Department of Transportation named the bridge in honor of Trooper Davis. The next town up the line on US 17 was Windsor, which is the hometown of Trooper Davis.

Chowan River basin and the Chowan County line at the Chowan River Bridge was the next point of interest and all day I was in and out of clouds and beautiful blue skies and white puffy clouds that turned into darker clouds with a few raindrops. There was no rain of any great magnitude after that very first shower I went through near Columbia, South Carolina. As I rode closer to my destination, some of the clouds started getting thick and getting a little dark, but I could still see blue sky behind it, so I was thinking that I was in good shape.

The Chowan River Bridge carries US 17 over the Chowan River in North Carolina and connects Merry Hill and Edenton. It is a continuous steel bridge with a concrete cast deck with only 62 feet of clearance below the bridge at the highest point. The bridge was built in 1999, with two lanes in each direction separated by a concrete barrier. As I rode into Virginia, I found myself on that section of US 17 they call the Blue Star Memorial Highway. [2]

I did make it to Bayside Harley-Davidson® in Portsmouth, Virginia, but not before they closed for the night. I did get a photo op out front and I would have to rearrange travel plans the next day to go there when they opened, so Plan B was initiated.

I finally got to US 378

Papa's General Store

Conway
to reach
Myrtle
Beach

Harley
Shop
at the
Beach

Beach
House
H-D

Carolina
Coast
H-D

Beaufort
County
Line

Roanoke
River
National
Wildlife
Refuge

Chowan
County
Line

Chowan
River
Bridge

Blue Star
Memorial
Highway

Bayside
Harley-
Davidson®

Day 2

Plan

Day	Starting Point / Ending Point	Miles / Ride Time	Potential Lodging	Potential Dining at Destination	Potential Attractions En Route
2 (Fri, Jul 10)	Portsmouth, VA Salisbury, MD	348 7:19	Motel 6 Salisbury, MD	The Greene Turtle Sports Bar & Grille; Your Pie	• Breakfast at Hometown Diner (Take-out); • Photo Op at Hampton Roads H-D (Prior to opening) • Lunch at Horne's, Port Royal, VA (Take-out); • Gas up at Horne's in Port Royal; • Gas up near Bridgeville, DE; • Rommel H-D – Delmarva, Salisbury, MD (If before 1900) Check first; • Motel 6, Salisbury; • U.S. 50 Endpoint Photo Op; • Motel 6, Salisbury

Actual

Day	Starting Point / Ending Point	Miles / Ride Time	Lodging	Dining at Destination	Attractions En Route
2 (Fri, Jul 10)	Portsmouth, VA Salisbury, MD	348 7:19	Motel 6 Salisbury, MD	Victoria's Crab House, Ocean City, MD	• Gas up at Shell, Portsmouth, VA; • Breakfast at Waffle House, Portsmouth, VA; • Bayside H-D, Portsmouth, VA (opened a register for me an hour early); • Photo Op at Hampton Roads H-D (Prior to opening); • Lunch at Horne's, Port Royal, VA (Dine-In); • All American H-D, Hughesville, MD; • Gas up at Shell, Hughesville, MD; • Rommel H-D – Delmarva, Salisbury, MD • Motel 6, Salisbury; • U.S. 50 Endpoint Photo Op, Ocean City, MD; • Dinner at Victoria's Crab House, Ocean City, MD (Dine-out); • Motel 6, Salisbury

Well, in Portsmouth, I had planned to go to the Hometown Diner, but it was closed or no longer in business, or so it seemed, so I went to the Waffle House and was served by a nice young lady by the name of Tabitha. I had my All-Star breakfast and ate the whole thing. One of the other servers at Waffle House liked my mask (there was a requirement to wear a mask to enter). I had made some masks for my trip. So, I gave her one of the Americana type that I made to match the do rags. She was very appreciative.

I got to Bayside Harley Davidson a little after 8:00 in the morning on Friday and met up with "Test Ride Rick", which was emblazoned in bold letters across his shirt, who said, "Come on in" as he pulled up on his bike and walked toward the front door. I got with Abby, who is the manager for the motorclothes, and she allowed me to get a shirt and poker chips even though it was technically before opening time. So, it was 8:42 and I was done and headed out towards Hampton Roads before Bayside officially opened!

As Day 2 actual travel started off heading into Isle of Wight County in Virginia still on US 17, I recollected some of my Virginia history I studied growing up in the Richmond, Virginia area, just ninety miles or so upstream of this part of the James River. [3]

Crossing the James River Bridge from Carrollton to Newport News, Virginia, I was reminded of working at Newport News Shipbuilding and Drydock Company during the summer of 1977 in the Submarine Test Department in the Weapons Test Group. Our assignment was to perform tests on the missile-bearing subs in for overhaul. The USS Ulysses S. Grant (SSBN-631) was the only one under overhaul at the time. SSBN stands for Submersible Ship Ballistic Nuclear and means that it is a submarine carrying ballistic missiles and is powered by a nuclear reactor. The number sequence falls under what is known as the 627-Class of submarines which began with the USS James Madison (SSBN-627). It was remarkably interesting living in Newport News that summer and I learned a lot about the workings of naval ships.

I stayed in the third-floor apartment of a house that was owned by a lady named Sophie Keel on 32nd Street in Newport News. That street ended at the docks where the carrier Eisenhower (CVN 69), the second in the Nimitz (CVN 68) class carrier series, was in dock being outfitted for commissioning that summer. So, at the end of my street, just on the other side of the chain-link fence, was this huge V-shaped hull of the carrier, which, come to think of it, was pretty awesome. Working at Newport News was a neat scenario, with working hours of seven-to-four with an hour for lunch. Living close enough to walk home, go to my third-floor balcony, after cooking some dinner and sit there and watch all the folks rush to get home made it all the more enjoyable. Anyway, that was that was an interesting summer, watching that carrier being outfitted at the end of my street.

The shipyard had an open house before the commissioning of the Eisenhower, and the commissioning folks gave out a sheet of information for the public to be made aware of all that the Eisenhower brought to the fleet. The handout outlined the parts and pieces and facts about the ship like there are three galleys that serve over thirty-five hundred sailors that are assigned to the ship and 18 levels, etc. But the neatest piece of information that sticks with me was that it has four-and-a-half acres of flight deck. So, that is the one thing that, to this day, still amazes me. [4] [5]

I got back on schedule Friday morning, even though it was a late departure because of needing to go by Bayside Harley-Davidson®, but they did open early for me. I made it to Hampton Roads Harley-Davidson® just for a photo op (no shirt or poker chips) because it was before they opened for the day, but I did get the picture for the Ride 365 program. The weather started out just beautiful and it was really good to see a lot of white puffy clouds and blue skies.

Again, my Virginia history schooling kicked in as I rode through Yorktown on US 17. In fourth grade, our class field trip was to Williamsburg and we also traveled down to Yorktown to see where the American forces defeated Cornwallis at the battle of Yorktown.

As it turns out, there is a maybe not-so-well-known story about the battle where Cornwallis was allegedly holed up in a cave in fear of his life. That cave is now known as "Cornwallis' Cave" and is located on Water Street on the waterfront in Yorktown. As a kid, it was always cool to think of this British general cowering in a cave from the American freedom fighters. [6] [7] [8]

From Yorktown, the crossing of the York River was on the George P. Coleman Bridge on US 17. [9] Then, riding through Gloucester County, I was reminded that this was the high school stomping grounds for Stacey Owens, a friend from over in Columbia, SC. She used to work at the Quaker Steak & Lube® and we met when they used to have Bike Nights there. I would get to as many bike nights as I could when I was working near there at the failed VC Summer nuclear plant construction. But I digress.

Continuing riding on US 17 in Virginia, I had the goal of getting almost to Fredericksburg to Port Royal, Virginia, where I would pick up US 301 to continue northward, the clouds were still white and puffy, and the blue sky was behind them. It was a great riding day for sure. [10]

Once again, my Virginia history kicked in and I remembered we studied about the geography of Virginia and the three big peninsulas of the state that start with the James River to the South and then a peninsula, then the York River, then a peninsula, then the Rappahannock River, then the Northern Neck and finally, the Potomac River between Virginia and the Maryland / Washington, D.C. area. [11]

Deciding to take a little side trip to All American Harley-Davidson® over in Hughesville, Maryland was a spur of the moment decision that was worthwhile. I decided to get a shirt, poker chips and a photo-op. The little detour turned out to be a good side trip.

US 50 and US 301 join up near Annapolis, Maryland and I crossed over the Chesapeake Bay Bridge with them together. I had been on this route before when I was riding up to Boston for a meeting and I had completed the northern part of US 301 from this point on to its terminus at that time in Glasgow, Delaware. Since then, the terminus is listed as Biddles Corner, Delaware, a little southeast of Glasgow.

Taking Maryland 404 to Delaware 404 to see another state along the route, I was able to see the beautiful farmland that turned out to be a very nice ride. That part of Maryland and Delaware has all sorts of crops, especially corn, that you would not normally associate with the Eastern Shore area without knowing about it beforehand. I could see my shadow getting longer and the corn getting taller as I headed back into Maryland from Delaware and then checked into the hotel in Salisbury. Before it became dark, I went ahead and jumped on US 50 headed East to Ocean City for a photo-op there. While in downtown, I got a few photos and reached the end point so I could get a shot of the sign that read US 50 goes West from this point.

Dinner was a great set of crab cakes at Victoria's Crab House in Ocean City, MD and were out of this world delicious. The folks there were absolutely as nice as could be. Coping with the COVID-19 restrictions, they did open air dining where you received a take-out box and found a socially distant table. After that wonderful dinner, I asked where I could obtain some picture post cards. They mentioned a shop on the boardwalk may have them, so I set off to that shop and bought five post cards of the same photo.

I should mention "my thing" about post cards here. Something I started doing years ago, when I only had one granddaughter, would be to always send post cards to her from the interesting places along my travel routes. This was especially true when I was on my bike traveling on a long trip or for a weekend riding excursion. It just became something for the two of us to share. She still has a shoe box full of them, which covers at least fifteen years. I now have 12 grandchildren, so for this trip, all three of the families agreed that I should only send one postcard per family instead of one for each child over two-years-old. I was beginning to appreciate more and more not having to write out nine post cards for each point of interest I came across during my travels as was the custom the last trip I took on the motorcycle.

Having eaten a good meal and acquired the necessary number of post cards, I set out for the hotel back in Salisbury, and was treated to a surprisingly picturesque sunset that God painted on the clouds.

James
River
Bridge

Hampton
Roads
Harley-
Davidson®

George P.
Coleman
Bridge

US 17 and
US 301 at
Port
Royal

Northern Neck of Virginia

All American Harley-Davidson®

Chesapeake
Bay Bridge

Riding
Delaware
404

Nearing US 50's endpoint in Ocean City

US 50 begins heading West

Crab Cakes at
Victoria's Crab House
in Ocean City, MD

US 50
back to
Salisbury

Plan

Day	Starting Point / Ending Point	Miles / Ride Time	Potential Lodging	Potential Dining at Destination	Potential Attractions En Route
3 (Sat, July 11)	Salisbury, MD Bridgeport, WV	350 8:27	Quality Inn Bridgeport – Clarksburg; Days Inn Bridgeport - Clarksburg; Best Western Plus - Bridgeport;	Mountaineer Grille; Eat'n Park; Parkette Family Restaurant; Toni's Ice Cream	• Breakfast at Royal Farms, Salisbury, MD (Take-out); • Rommel H-D, Annapolis, MD (Photo op only prior to opening); • Gas up in Annapolis; • Winchester H-D, Winchester; • Gas up in Winchester; • Early Lunch at Bonnie Blue Southern Market & Bakery, Winchester (Visit Mary Himelright, et. al.) (Must leave Bonnie Blue by 11:30); • RG's Almost Heaven Harley-Davidson®, Clarksburg, WV (if before 1600)

Actual

Day	Starting Point / Ending Point	Miles / Ride Time	Lodging	Dining at Destination	Attractions En Route
3 (Sat, July 11)	Salisbury, MD Bridgeport, WV	350 8:27	Sleep Inn, Bridgeport – Clarksburg	Eat'n Park (Dine-In);	• Breakfast at Royal Farms, Salisbury, MD (Take-out); • Gas up in Salisbury, MD; • Winchester H-D, Winchester, VA; • Gas up at Shell in Winchester, VA; • Lunch at Bonnie Blue Southern Market & Bakery, Winchester, VA (Dine-In); • RG's Almost Heaven Harley-Davidson® (Photo Op only) Clarksburg, WV; • Supper at Eat 'n Park (Dine-In); • Mass Online – Adelaide, Australia

So, on Saturday, July 11th, I left Salisbury, Maryland, a little later than I expected, but it worked out just fine. I went to Royal Farms, which is a convenience store/gas station type of place, but they had some good food there. It was a takeout only, so I got a good breakfast sandwich and took it out, sat on the curb next to the bike and had my breakfast. When I was done, a fella came up to me and says, "Where are you going?". I told him, and he asked, "Why do you want to do that?" and I gave him one of my business cards I had printed to support the Ride for Kids® (http://www.curethekids.org/) and he said, "Well, I can't keep the card because

I'll lose it, but I'll make a donation." He then went into his truck and gathered up some cash and stuck it in my hand and said, "Just remember me as the wandering soul." I will have to document that somehow. He was a nice guy, for sure.

I started out on US 50 headed West from there now towards the Chesapeake Bay Bridge again, but in the opposite direction, first crossing over the Nanticoke River Memorial Bridge near Vienna, Maryland. The Nanticoke River Memorial Bridge near Vienna, Maryland was rededicated on May 30, 2016, in memory of those from Dorchester and Wicomico counties who served in combat during World War I.

The first of several Harriet Tubman commemorative markers along my journey shows up on this section of US 50. Two other states had references to her in one form or another. Later in the book, on US 20 up in the northeast, markers also talk about Harriet Tubman because she had a home up there in Auburn, New York. More on that later.

Entering the town of Easton, Maryland was interesting in that it was a combination of the old and the new. [12]

And then I proceeded to take US 50 back across the Bay Bridge and into Annapolis, into Washington, D.C. and encountering more construction. This time it was with the motorcycle warning at the at the beginning of the Chesapeake Bay Bridge. Crossing the Bay again from the opposite direction was still very interesting as I do enjoy large bodies of water. So, I was back crossing the Bay Bridge again and closing in on Annapolis and Washington, D.C., and the Severn River Bridge. [13]

In Washington, DC, there was construction going on, so naturally, you cannot always get to where you want to go when you want to go there, but I was able to at least trace through all parts of U.S. 50 that are in D.C. US 50 comes into Washington, DC on New York Avenue, then down 6th Street towards Constitution Avenue. Turning right onto Constitution Avenue, it continues toward the shared bridge with Interstate 66, where it crosses the Potomac River into Virginia. Shortly after crossing the Potomac, US 50 takes you into Fairfax, Virginia. There is a photo that shows the City Welcome Sign as I waited for the light to change.

The town of Fairfax - I could not help but remember it as the city where my father passed away 12 years prior. He was on the way back from a trip to Florida to see my sister. He and my mom drove their car to the train station - one of those arrangements where they put your car on the train, and you also ride the train. He got sick before getting to Fairfax and would not impose on anybody else to stop the train, before getting to the endpoint near Fairfax. He ended up in the hospital there.

We learned about Dad about seven o'clock or so on Christmas Eve, so I just packed a bike backpack and jumped on the bike and took off. I took the bike because, at that time, we had two vehicles, a car, and my bike. I got as far as Roanoke Rapids, North Carolina, and was hoping to get to Virginia, but it was little after midnight and a downpour came. Of course, being dark, you really do not know what is going on with the weather until it is on top of you, so I got soaked and stopped there. I checked in and then I hung everything up and dried everything out. I got up early the next morning and headed on up to the hospital in Fairfax.

It was early Christmas morning when I arrived there, so I just waited to see when my mother would show up. As I later learned, she had stayed overnight with my cousin and her husband at their house in Reisterstown, Maryland. They came in as I was just standing there in the waiting room with my leathers on just waiting. Then I see this gentleman wheeling up a lady in a wheelchair and my cousin was behind him. I said, "Wait a minute, that's my Mom!" I had never seen her being transported in a wheelchair before. Not to belabor that issue, they did not recognize me at first and I did not recognize them at first. When we realized who we were, respectively, we had a surprised exchange. That day, I did see my father before he passed away, and I stayed with my mom for a few days there. So, entering the town of Fairfax brought back a bittersweet memory.

Leaving Fairfax, I encountered the first of the many roundabouts lots of different states are using now too to control traffic instead of traffic lights and traffic signals. Obviously, it is less maintenance, and it keeps things moving when there is not a whole lot of traffic and folks do not really have to stop for everybody else. I have tried to capture a few of those along the way so there is a montage of roundabouts in the back of the book.

Aldie, Virginia is one of several small towns along US 50 coming from Fairfax headed towards Winchester, Virginia. It was a pleasant day riding through Aldie, Virginia, which has two historical markers that read as follows:

"In June 1863, Gen. Robert E. Lee led the Army of Northern Virginia through gaps in the nearby Blue Ridge Mountains and into the Shenandoah Valley to invade the North. Maj. Gen. J.E.B. Stuart's cavalry corps screened the army from Federal observation. The Union cavalry commander, Brig. Gen. Alfred Pleasonton attempted to break through Stuart's screen, and fought three sharp engagements along this road. They included the Battles of Aldie (17 June), Middleburg (19 June), and Upperville (21 June). Stuart fell back westward under Pleasonton's pressure but kept the Federal cavalry east of the gaps. "

"In this vicinity (and according to tradition two miles east at Peach Orchard) was born Julia Beckwith Neale, mother of Stonewall Jackson, February 29, 1798. She married Johnathan Jackson in 1818 and died, October 1831." [14]

One could spend all day in this little town due to the history and the connection to other parts of the country, which will be mentioned later as we get into another state simply because it is part of some history from this location.

I remember going through Middleburg often and wanting to participate in some of the horse sports activities, but never availed myself of the opportunity. [15]

The little town of Upperville was, in my memory, a town of high-income residents who had big farms and horses. [16]

I then made my way to Winchester Harley-Davidson® and met a nice young lady there by the name of Autumn Rain and gave her a Ride for Kids® card and said take a look. She said she would visit the website. I picked out my poker chips and then went outside to capture my photo op for Ride 365. It was so windy that it would blow the tripod down, so I had to shorten the stick and not have it up so high and then it worked out all right.

Entering Winchester, Virginia, a city which has grown exponentially since I went to high school there in the early 70's was, for me, a little nostalgic as well as remembering history.

The historical parts have remained and include:

Fort Loudoun – the site of George Washington's regimental headquarters during the French and Indian War;

George Washington Office Museum – was a military office from September 1755 to December of 1756 while Fort Loudoun was being constructed;

Stonewall Jackson's Headquarters – contains the largest collection of Jackson memorabilia;

Abram's Delight – the site of five generations of the prominent Hollingsworth family covering 200 years;

Handley Regional Library – Judge John Handley of Scranton, Pennsylvania left $250,000 in his will to " . . . open a Public Library for the free use of the people of the city of Winchester forever.";

The Patsy Cline Historic House – on the National Register of Historic Places and the Virginia Landmarks Register;

The Stewart Bell Jr. Archives – located in the basement of the Handley Regional Library Headquarters, houses an extensive collection of materials on the people, places, and events of lower Shenandoah Valley from 1732 to present. (I went to church with Stewart Bell – he was my father's friend) [17] [18]

US 50 enters Winchester from the East on Millwood Pike which becomes Millwood Avenue and passes by the George Washington Office Museum on the right, which is just a little building you would miss if not for the signage indicating the location. I then went over to Bonnie Blue Southern Market & Bakery and had a great lunch, a Cuban sandwich with their special seasoned fries they have, and it was exceptionally good. I was served by a nice young lady named Lily who was interested in the Ride for Kids®, so I gave her a card and she said she would look it up. Hopefully, the word gets out about the Ride for Kids® because they really need our help to continue their valiant effort to find a cure for childhood brain tumors. I tried to make contact with some of my friends that live in Winchester, but nobody was able to meet up for lunch due to COVID-19.

After that great lunch, I then rode by my old high school building, which is right on US 50, James Wood High School. The building is now a middle school and they basically have two high schools in the county whereas, when I went to school it was only James Wood for the whole of Frederick County.

Continuing heading West, I got to the West Virginia State line stating, "Wild Wonderful West Virginia" and then into Romney, West Virginia. Officially chartered in 1762, Romney is one of the two oldest cities in West Virginia. Not far out of town is one of the nation's best-preserved Civil War trenches at Fort Mill Ridge. [19]

After Romney, US 50 takes you across that little tip of Maryland that comes down for only a few-mile stretch and then back into West Virginia, so that made it a little more interesting. At this point, clouds were starting to develop to take out the blue sky, but later dissipated. I did start to see blue skies again before I reached Clarksburg, West Virginia. One direction into town basically looked like you were going through a parking garage and when you were going under it, the sign says, "Home of Jimbo Fisher". Jimbo Fisher, who led Florida State University to a national championship in 2013, was named head football coach at Texas A&M University on December 4, 2017.

There is another entrance to Clarksburg that garners the chain link fence type of signage connections for all of the civic groups that are part of that town. I then stopped in at Almost Heaven Harley-Davidson® for only a photo op there since it was after hours.

"Clarksburg is the birthplace of General Thomas J. 'Stonewall' Jackson." [20]

Remember Stonewall Jackson's mother was born in Aldie, Virginia?

After I went through Clarksburg, West Virginia, I ended up in Bridgeport, because that was where the hotels were, and I needed a place to stay after a long day riding.

After checking into the hotel, I reflected on my last part of US 50 heading toward Clarksburg. I can understand why the GPS folks and the Google Maps folks do not route you on U.S. 50 from Romney to Grafton. There is a big stretch in there between Gormania, West Virginia and I think it is Maryland 560 that goes off to the right and US 50 goes to the left. From that point to about five miles from Grafton, West Virginia, it was a terrible road, absolutely terrible. I mean, washboard type surfaces, you know, potholes filled with stuff that have potholes that are filled with stuff, multiple layers and levels of pavement crumbling and all sorts of things. Just not really maintained much at all in that part of Maryland or West Virginia. So, had I not wanted to specifically go on Route 50, I would not have chosen that particular stretch of the road.

I made it to Grafton, stopped and got a snack, and since it was only about 15 miles from where I was going to end up anyway, it was a good time to take a break. I took a little tour through Clarksburg and slipped into RG's Almost Heaven Harley-Davidson®, which was closed. I knew it was going to be closed because I set out that morning a little too late to get there earlier. I made my photo op there and then proceeded to go to the Quality Inn in Bridgeport. For dinner I walked down to the "Eat'n Park", which offered an incredibly good burger, a mushroom and onion burger, and I met a nice young lady there serving by the name of Angie. I had dinner and then got some milk and cookies to go so, I could have some milk and cookies for a snack later. After that, my activity was copying the photos from the dash cam to the laptop to prepare for the next day's photos.

Realizing that my original plans for attending Mass at the various locations either Saturday night or Sunday morning would not always work since the onset of COVID-19 would make it unpredictable at best, I decided to search for online Masses. That way, I could attend and partake in a spiritual communion and not have to be dependent on whether or not churches would be open at the times I needed, either Saturday night or Sunday morning. That also meant that I would not have to invoke the travel dispensation over four Sundays, and I really did not want to do that. Tonight, I "traveled" to Adelaide, Australia to go to Mass which was a great experience. Then it was really time to go to sleep.

Chesapeake
Bay Bridge

Severn
River
Bridge

US 50
turns
down 6th
Street in
D.C.

US 50 on
Constitution
Avenue in
D.C.

Fairfax, Virginia

Aldie, Virginia

Middleburg,
Virginia

Upperville,
Virginia

Winchester Harley-Davidson®

George Washington Office Museum

Bonnie
Blue
Southern
Market &
Bakery

Original
James
Wood
High
School
Building

Romney, West Virginia

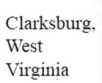

Clarksburg, West Virginia

Day 4

Plan

Day	Starting Point / Ending Point	Miles / Ride Time	Potential Lodging	Potential Dining at Destination	Potential Attractions En Route
4a (Sun, July 12)	Bridgeport, WV Seymour, IN	364 7:32			• Breakfast at Hardee's, 722 E Main St, Clarksburg, WV (Take-out); • 0800 Mass at Immaculate Conception; • Old Canal Smoke House for lunch, Chillicothe, OH (Dine-In); • Gas up in Chillicothe; • Hopewell Culture National Historical Park, Chillicothe, OH; • Seip Mound, Paxton Township, OH; • Slip into KY across Roebling Bridge to Roebling Murals
4b (Sun, July 12)	Seymour, IN Lexington, IN	34 0:41	Matt & Karen's		

Actual

Day	Starting Point / Ending Point	Miles / Ride Time	Lodging	Dining at Destination	Attractions En Route
4 (Sun, July 12)	Bridgeport, WV Lexington, IN	398 8:13	Matt & Karen's	Matt & Karen's	• Breakfast at hotel; • Gas up in Bridgeport; • Old Canal Smoke House for lunch, Chillicothe, OH (Dine-In); • Gas up in Chillicothe, OH; • Seip Mound, Paxton Township, OH;

It was a beautiful day with blue skies and wispy white clouds and wide-open spaces as I rolled into Parkersburg, West Virginia. That is, until crossing the Ohio River when the rain started. It was never a hard rain, but enough to be a nuisance and get you wet over a long time if you did not put on the rain gear. So, after crossing into Ohio, the rain gear had to go on. It was just a misty drizzle, but over time it would certainly soak you.

Parkersburg, by the way was originally named Newport in the late 18th century following the American Revolutionary War. The town area was laid out on land granted to Alexander Parker for his Revolutionary War service, and the area was renamed for him as Parkersburg in 1810. [21]

Entering Athens, Ohio, the county seat of Athens County, Ohio I learned that it was where Ohio University was located. [22]

I was going across town from one side to the other to get to The Athens Harley-Davidson® dealership and lo and behold I came across StewMac or Stuart McDonald as it was called back when I purchased banjo making and guitar making tools and materials. I had purchased many banjo parts from them when I built my banjo back in 1975. They were recommended to me by Andy Boorman, who was instrumental (no pun intended) in providing me with the incentive to build my banjo as well as selling me some parts. I do still have their planetary gearheads on that banjo, and it was just very neat to see the Stewart McDonald building there in Athens. I think I still have Catalog No. 7 from back then, when it was just a glossy paper center stapled and folded catalog of about a dozen pages or so. Now they have an enormous business dealing in musical instrument parts and luthier tools and supplies nationwide. [23]

So, I got a picture of the Stewart MacDonald building and then did my photo op over at the Athens Harley-Davidson® dealership.

Moving on from there, the clouds around did not really rain on me very much, but they just seemed to be swelling around and being threatening. Then I rode into where the clouds were breaking up and I was riding through the beautiful Ohio countryside sunshiny behind the clouds which looked very pretty. One cannot help but view in wonder how God created such beautiful landscape.

I finally made it to the Old Canal Smokehouse in Chillicothe, Ohio and met a nice young lady by the name of Heidi who was my server there. This was one of those days where spending some extra time cleaning the bike in the morning from the previous day's journey on Thursday, that became a wasted effort because, naturally, when I got ready to get on the two-lane part of US 50 right at Parkersburg, and it starts to rain across the river into Ohio. It was kind of spotty showers and nothing too bad till I got to the end of the four lane and it looked like it was going to get really bad. I stopped to put rain gear on. It was a good thing to do that because it would have been a long, wet ride to get here to Chillicothe, which is where the Old Canal Smokehouse is, so I stopped to eat lunch. Heidi's husband is ex-military and has a bike and she showed me the cool paint job he had on it. We had a great conversation and I left her a card for the Ride for Kids®.

Stopping by the Seip Indian mound, which is supposedly one of the largest built by the Hopewell culture there, I allowed the dash cam to take what would become the last photo of the day. [24]

This was the last dash cam photo for the day due to the threatening rain farther ahead, but I probably could have left the camera on the handlebar for my trip through Cincinnati. As I approached Cincinnati, it got really stormy and dark, so the rain gear went on and the camera went off and into the saddlebag. It all fizzled out when I actually got to Cincinnati. Oh well, that is how it goes sometimes.

I met up with my wife's cousin, Matt, who wanted to ride with me for a while, but his father had just passed away the week before, so family business was more important. We did get to ride a little while in Indiana to his house, where I spent the night. We went to see his mother and had a nice visit in spite of the circumstances.

When we returned from visiting Matt's mother, as we were checking the bikes as we entered the house through the garage, I found that I had lost one latch off of my tour pack on the back of the bike. Apparently, no Loctite® was used on the assembly of them. Matt had some blue Loctite® that he gave me, so I systematically removed each screw in the other latches and hinges, applied the Loctite® to each screw and replaced each back together. And that's the way it was that Sunday night.

Beautiful
Day in
West
Virginia

Crossing
the Ohio
River

Stewart-
MacDonald
Manufacturing,
Inc., Athens,
Ohio.

Athens
Harley-
Davidson®

Ohio
Countryside

Seip
Mound

Day 5

Plan

Day	Starting Point / Ending Point	Miles / Ride Time	Potential Lodging	Potential Dining at Destination	Potential Attractions En Route
5 (Mon, July 13)	Lexington, IN Union, MO	389 7:01	Super 8	Cowan's Restaurant; Tres Toritos; Junie Moon Café; Big Boys Pub & Subs	• Breakfast at Matt & Karen's; • Medora Covered Bridge, Medora, IN; • George Rogers Clark Memorial, Vincennes; • Gas up in Vincennes • Lunch at Five Brothers Café, Salem, IL (Take-out); • Green Mount Road H-D (formerly Frieze H-D), O'Fallon, IL; • Gas up in O'Fallon; • Gateway H-D, St. Louis, MO; • Historic U.S. 66 excursion • Honey Pit BBQ, Kirkwood, MO for turnaround spot for Route 66; • Route 66 State Park Visitor Center, Eureka, MO; • Route 66 State Park, Eureka, MO; • Historic Route 66, Villa Ridge, MO

Actual

Day	Starting Point / Ending Point	Miles / Ride Time	Lodging	Dining at Destination	Attractions En Route
5 (Mon, July 13)	Lexington, IN St. Louis, MO	389 7:01	Hampton Inn, St. Louis	Order in Imo's Pizza	• Breakfast at Matt & Karen's; • Gas up along the way to Louisville H-D; • H-D of Louisville for Tour Pak Latch; • Lunch at Larrison's Diner, Seymour, IN (Dine-In); • Medora Covered Bridge, Medora, IN; • George Rogers Clark Memorial, Vincennes, IN; • Gas up in Vincennes; • Green Mount Road H-D (formerly Frieze H-D), O'Fallon, IL; • Gateway H-D, St. Louis, MO (Photo op only); • Supper from Imo's Pizza (Take-out/Delivery)

A great sunny day leaving Matt and Karen's house heading out in Indiana to Harley-Davidson® Louisville because it just so happens that Harley-Davidson® Louisville was open on Monday, so I could check into acquiring a replacement latch. I was able to cross the Ohio River, which cost me a toll both ways, and go to the Harley-Davidson® dealer there bought my replacement latch with Tim Brinson helping me. I also got my poker chips with the help of Desiree Waddell. I also was able to get another photo op for the Ride 365 program for H.O.G.®

Meanwhile, I had bungee cords holding the lid on and rode up to Seymour and over to North Vernon to catch that stretch of US 50 that we missed when Matt met me on the road near Lawrenceburg. Anyway, I was back on track for the start of the day – the original plan – but it was one o'clock in the afternoon, so I was not sure I was going to get all the way to Union, Missouri. But it was a bright, sunny, beautiful day and not too hot yet.

Well, because of the change in plans on Monday, I did get to go to Larrison's Diner, for lunch instead of breakfast, and it was incredibly good. I had the biggest burger and their beer battered fried onion rings were out of this world. Great place for a great meal.

Matt had mentioned to me earlier in the month that I should consider a stop by the covered bridge near Medora, Indiana, so I made the little detour. The bridge is "the longest covered bridge in the USA." [25]

I continued on US 50 over to Vincennes, Indiana and actually had to go to Illinois first and come back into Indiana the way Route 50 was re-routed in years past. Anyway, I stopped in to see the George Rogers Clark National Historical Park and viewed the monument there. [26] I captured a few photos of the old cathedral and the French and Indian Cemetery historical marker that is there. Next, I needed to go back across the bridge, which is the Lincoln Memorial Bridge, that takes the old Route 50 across, but it had been re-routed to go another direction. It is still a beautiful sunny day not many clouds.

Originally, for Day 5, we were to leave out from Matt's, with another friend Randy, who lives around the Louisville area planning to ride a little bit on Route 50 from the area around Seymour, Indiana. Seymour is North of Lexington, which is North of New Albany which is the hometown of my wife's folks as well as Matt's. Breakfast was to be at Larrison's Diner near Seymour, but I decided since I was the only one on this trip at least I could eat lunch there.

I was later leaving so I was heading into the sun on US 50 and made the stop at O'Fallon, Illinois at Green Mount Road Harley-Davidson® to get a photo op there and collect my poker chips as well. While selecting my poker chips, I engaged in a conversation with a very pleasant lady by the name of Michelle, who is the Motorclothes Manager there. She was very helpful, and we had a genuinely nice conversation.

As I left O'Fallon, I was getting closer to Saint Louis and I started staring into the sun more and more, I could see the Gateway Arch in the distance. Since US 50 does not go into the major part of the city but drops down around the South side and swings around to pick up Interstate 35, that was about as close as I would get. That was just fine with me, because I had been up in it three times already and did not need to go a fourth.

Heading West from there, I did get to have a photo op of the "Gateway to the West" or Gateway Harley-Davidson® dealership there. They were closed, but that that was the way it goes, so I cut it short for that day and stayed in Saint Louis and figured I would pick up the pace the next day. While stopped at Gateway Harley Davidson for my photo op, a fellow on a bicycle came up and got to talking and he donated five dollars to the Ride for Kids®. So, I stuck it in my pouch to turn in later.

Since I was running behind, I decided to stay in the area for the night, so I went to the Hampton Inn down the way a little bit. And two nice ladies, Nancy, and Savannah, helped me check in and recommended a pizza delivery, so I ordered pizza and ate in my room.

The
Indiana
back
roads

Harley-
Davidson®
Louisville

Medora
Covered
Bridge,
Medora,
Indiana

Old
Cathedral
Catholic
Church

Old
Cathedral
Catholic
Church

George
Rogers
Clark
National
Historical
Park

The
Lincoln
Memorial
Bridge

Green
Mount
Road
Harley-
Davidson®

Entering
St. Louis

Gateway
Harley-
Davidson®

Plan

Day	Starting Point / Ending Point	Miles / Ride Time	Potential Lodging	Potential Dining at Destination	Potential Attractions En Route
6 (Tue, July 14)	Union, MO Ottawa, KS	264 4:36	Comfort Inn; Super 8; SureStay Hotel; Days Inn	Guy & Mae's Tavern (Take-out) (Williamsburg – 20 minutes from hotel down old Route 50); Freddy's Frozen Custard & Steakburgers; Old 56 Family Restaurant	• Breakfast at Junie Moon Café (Take-out); • Clark's Hill/ Norton State Historic Site, Jefferson City, MO; • Lunch at Kehde's Barbeque, Sedalia, MO (Take-out); • Yeager's Cycle Sales, Sedalia, MO; • Gas up in Sedalia • Whiteman AFB, Knob Noster, MO; • Tribute To Old Drum, Warrensburg, MO; • Rawhide H-D, Olathe, KS; • Old Depot Museum, Ottawa, KS; • (Laundry Day – South Main Coin Laundry)

Actual

Day	Starting Point / Ending Point	Miles / Ride Time	Lodging	Dining at Destination	Attractions En Route
6 (Tue, July 14)	St. Louis, MO Ottawa, KS	299 5:24	Days Inn	Freddy's Frozen Custard & Steakburgers; Old 56 Family Restaurant;	• Breakfast at Hotel; • Route 66 State Park Visitor Center, Eureka, MO; • Route 66 State Park, Eureka, MO; • Gas stop in Eureka, MO; • Lunch at Bandanas Barbeque, Sedalia, MO (Dine-In); • Yeager's Cycle Sales, Sedalia, MO; • Gas up in Sedalia • Rawhide H-D, Olathe, KS; • Supper from Freddy's Frozen Custard & Steakburgers (Take-out);

Ok, so Tuesday, the 14th, I was setting out to head west again and had thirty-five miles to make up because I had to stay in St. Louis instead of Union, Missouri. Missouri actually has a Route 66 State Park, so I did a little detour there and went up to the visitor center. The GPS does not help a whole lot in this case, because it wants to take you through a quarry road that was not a public throughway. So, you have to kind of point out on the map a particular point in between where you are and where you want to go before it actually gets you there. I went around my elbow to get to my knee, so to speak, but I found both sides of the park. Of course, the visitor center was closed due to the COVID-19 issue, but I did get some dash cam pictures of it. I was able get into the other part of the park another way and found the old section of Route 66 bridge that is in the process of being restored. I then rolled on some part of the old historic Route 66 Road [27] that was part of the park and that was fun. It was a sunshiny wispy white cloud day and very nice riding weather, but after I got back on the road, I got behind another box.

Missouri has scenic farm country like all the other states and as I moved further West, clouds started to cover up a lot more of the sky. It was less of the blue sky there and more of the not so dark kind of clouds in the sky. Then it started to look like it was going to possibly rain again, but I never did need to put rain gear on from that point on. God is good to me a lot in that regard.

As I motored on toward Sedalia, Missouri I noticed a marker for the Scott Joplin Memorial Highway. Scott Joplin sometimes stayed in that area and there is an interesting, but somewhat sad story related to Sedalia. You might remember Scott Joplin as the music composer for much of the movie, "The Sting", but he did much more than just that music, "….music that Joplin had composed more than a half-century earlier…." [28]

Sedalia is also home to the Scott Joplin Ragtime Festival, an annual event promoting classical ragtime music pioneered by Scott Joplin in the early 1900's. The festival is held in late May to early June each year drawing crowds from all over the country to enjoy his style of music. [29]

Well, one other great thing in Sedalia is Bandanas Barbeque. It was awesome. I had the beef brisket there and it was particularly good. Meghan was the server, and she did an excellent job. So, for me, Bandanas is a "go to" place from now on if I ever get to Sedalia again. Part of the motif is that red, white, and blue bandanas are hanging on pipes all around the dining area to create a curtain effect between booths. Very clever, indeed.

After lunch, I rode through downtown Sedalia in several loops around on different streets to get some good pictures on the dash cam. Rain was just kind of threatening all around, but it just did not really do much, so I did not see any need to put rain gear on for sure. I rode over to the Katy Line Railroad Station, which has become the visitor center. The rail line is nicknamed Katy because it is really the Missouri-Kansas-Texas railroad, the K-T, or the Katy. There is some history about the railroad in the visitor center and I was able to obtain some post cards to send to the grandkids. [30] [31] The depot now serves as the visitor and information center for Sedalia.

In another part of town, I checked in with Yeager's Harley-Davidson® for my poker chips and photo op. I had to work at a good set up for the photo op, but I did find an angle that worked in the end. After that, it was time for this old man to hit the road again.

As I was moving closer to Kansas, I got to see some white clouds and blue skies as well as bug splatter on the windshield. I did make it to Olathe, Kansas and stopped in at Rawhide Harley-Davidson®, picked out a T shirt and poker chips and went ahead and got another latch for the tour pack, just to make sure. Then I left out of Olathe and headed to Ottawa, Kansas for the night and of course got myself behind another box along the way.

Once in Ottawa, I had a little time to work on the Tour-Pak latch. Staying at the Days Inn, the parking lot backed up to the Walmart parking lot, so I walked over to Walmart to pick up a tool to cut off screws for the fit-up. Making sure to apply the Loctite® to all threaded parts before reassembly. Mission accomplished in time to get everything buttoned up before the little bit of rain came through town for the overnight.

Route 66
State Park
Visitor
Center

Section
of Old
Route 66
Bridge

Route 66
bridge
Photo
Op

Part of
the Old
Mother
Road

Scott
Joplin
Memorial
Highway

Bandanas
Barbeque
in Sedalia,
MO

Downtown Sedalia, Missouri

The Katy Line Station of the M-K-T Line

Plan

Day	Starting Point / Ending Point	Miles / Ride Time	Potential Lodging	Potential Dining at Destination	Potential Attractions En Route
7 (Wed, July 15)	Ottawa, KS Dodge City, KS	289 4:44	Wyatt Earp Hotel; Quality Inn; Comfort Suites; Town Place Suites	Billy Sims Barbecue; Inn Pancake House; Dodge City Brewing; Central Station Bar & Grill	• Breakfast at Old 56 Family Restaurant, Ottawa, KS (Dine-In); • Strong City Depot & Railroad Park, Strong, KS; • Chase County Courthouse, Cottonwood Falls, KS; • Lunch at The Breadbasket, Newton, KS (Delivery); • Gas up in Newton; • Warkentin House, Newton, KS; • Mills Avenue photo op somewhere between Hutchinson and Prevna, KS; • Midway Sign, Kinsley, KS (photo op on west side near 56 jct west); • Most Wanted H-D, Dodge City, KS (if before 1700); • Historic Santa Fe Depot, Dodge City; • Doc Holliday Statue; • Boot Hill Museum; • Boot Hill Distillery

Actual

Day	Starting Point / Ending Point	Miles / Ride Time	Lodging	Dining at Destination	Attractions En Route
7 (Wed, July 15)	Ottawa, KS Dodge City, KS	289 4:44	Wyatt Earp Hotel	Casa Alvarez; Dodge House Restaurant	• Breakfast at Old 56 Family Restaurant, Ottawa, KS (Dine-In); • (Laundry Day – At Days Inn) • Gas stop at Emporia, KS; • Lunch at The Breadbasket, Newton, KS (Dine-In); • Warkentin House, Newton, KS; • Gas up in Offerle, KS (Down to fumes); • Most Wanted H-D, Dodge City, KS: • Rode through/around town with dash cam on; • Casa Alvarez for supper (Dine-In)

Day seven rolled around and I woke up in Ottawa, Kansas that morning with the weather being a little bit rainy in that area. It had rained overnight, and it was still a little rainy in the morning. I said to myself "OK,

I'll get up and be at the laundromat at seven thirty when they open, get my laundry done, go eat breakfast, get packed up and get out of town." I was trying to find the laundromat because I could not do laundry the night before since I fixed the Tour-Pak latch. I could not get into the laundromat, at least not the one that was supposed to be at that location. I got there before seven thirty and nobody showed up, so I left there at eight o'clock and went back to the hotel. It is walking distance from the restaurant, so I put stuff back in the room, and decided to go eat breakfast.

Breakfast was at the Old 56 Family Restaurant, which was exceptionally good. The server there, Kim, was genuinely nice and she was trying to tell me there was another laundromat because I told her what I had done. As I was walking back to my room after breakfast, lo and behold there was a washer and two dryers in the ice and vending area, so I decided to just do laundry there. Instead of picking it up and taking it somewhere, I could stay there and do laundry. With laundry completed and repacked, I checked out at eleven thirty, which put me way behind getting down the road. I still managed to make it to the most wanted Harley-Davidson® in Dodge City, Kansas before dark.

Heading out leaving Ottawa and the rain behind I continued heading West and it was a nice sunny day, but then as I got closer to Emporia, Kansas it was beginning to get cloudy, but no more rain. Emporia has a little history with bicycles. [32]

It is kind of interesting that roundabouts are out on the Kansas Plains and there is a page in the back of the book with a few photos of them. I was blessed with blue skies and white puffies along with some white wispys. As the white puffies got bigger and darker I got behind another box and rode through another roundabout before reaching Newton, KS. It is a nice little town and there was a lot of railroad stuff and then there was some interesting old gunfighter type information. There is a nice write-up there in the link at the back of the book to get you information about downtown Newton Kansas. [33] [34]

Traveling on the Chisholm Trail was an interesting part of Route 50 as it came through Newton, Kansas. [35] [36] Another historical part of Newton is the Sand Creek Station Golf Course. [37]

I had lunch at the Breadbasket, which was a really great bread focused restaurant. I believe it is Mennonite and they really do make bread that is just awesome. I had a splendidly prepared Philly Cheese Steak sandwich there and they had an open table of breads that they had baked, and you got what you want and ate what you took. Exceptionally good breads were served all day long.

After lunch, I rode through Newton a little bit and got behind a box again, but that was really short-lived. Approaching the famous Warkentin House in Newton, Kansas, I caught some dash cam shots. [38]

The historical marker at the Warkentin House reads:

BERNHARD WARKENTIN

"This Victorian house was built for Bernhard and Wilhelmina Warkentin in 1886-87. Bernhard was born in 1847 in the Mennonite village of Altonau, Ukraine. His father was a prominent miller. In 1872 he came to the U.S. to find new land. His letters home made him a leader of the Mennonite migration from Russia; about 5000 Mennonites came to Kansas. In 1875 he married Wilhelmina Eisenmayer, from a German Methodist family in Illinois. Her father was also a miller. In Kansas, Warkentin operated several mills and promoted wheat growing, especially "Turkey Red" hard winter wheat. His work helped make Kansas the "Bread Basket of the World." He died by accidental gunshot on a trip in the Holy Land in 1908. Wilhelmina lived here until her death in 1932. The house is on the National Register of Historic Places." [39]

Grain, and more specifically, wheat has become the mainstay of this area of Kansas. Over 40% of the wheat grown in this country is grown in Kansas.

Then I got back out onto the Kansas Plains and it was really picturesque out there with wide-open flat country for sure. Believe it or not, out in the Kansas Plains there is a roundabout! As I was just riding through there for little bit, I just found myself singing one of the old John Denver songs where he had an uncle name of Matthew, so that was always an interesting thing to do – sing to myself. I actually sang to myself a lot on this trip and it was a fun pastime.

"…..Gold is just a windy Kansas wheat-field
and blue is just a Kansas summer sky
And blue was just a Kansas summer sky…."
- John Denver, Lyrics from "Matthew"

Moving along farther West I got to Kinsley, Kansas, which is touted as the halfway point between New York and Los Angeles. They used to have a big major sign there that said 1544 miles this way to LA and 1544 miles back that way to New York, but that was when roads were a lot different than they are now. Who knows where the real center of the country is, but that is their claim to fame. From Kinsley, I got to a long stretch of road where I thought there was supposed to be a gas station within 8 miles or something like that, according to the Google Maps GPS. I went a whole lot farther than 8 miles and I started getting a little bit concerned because I was way out in the middle of nowhere and I thought I was running on fumes. I did make it to Offerle, Kansas and there was one gas station there and that is where I got gas. Thank God for the Offerle Country Store! Offerle is between Kinsley and Dodge City and there are miles and miles of wind generators out there. I am not sure how much they really produce, but there are a whole lot of them covering that wide area out there. Along that stretch of US 50, I was in and out of the clouds and blue skies and there were also some white puffies and dark bottom white puffies, which all in all made for a good ride.

When I went into Dodge City, I could see at one of the entrances the silhouettes of the Boot Hill gunslingers, at least, that is what I call them. I think it is just kind of a marketing tool to promote Dodge City. Next, I stopped in at Most Wanted Harley-Davidson®, got a T-shirt, poker chips and a photo op. While there I talked with some good folks as well, so it was fun and then I checked into my hotel for the night. It was the Wyatt Earp Hotel. It carries the name even though it is not much to look at as it is just pretty much a big box of a house, nothing fancy. The rooms were very rustic, with wood log beds and framework, so it was fun just to stay at the Wyatt Earp Hotel in Dodge City, Kansas. Before I forget, the lady that checked me in at the Wyatt Earp Hotel was named Libda, a name of someone I had known before, back in Augusta.

After unloading and putting my stuff up in the room, I wanted to take off just to ride around town for a little bit and see the sights because the sun had not gone completely down yet. I went out to the bike and an interesting and potentially panic situation at the hotel developed. I have two key fobs that interact with the security and start circuits of the bike allowing the start button to start the engine. One I kept in my jacket pocket and one I kept in my jeans pocket for the times I needed to access the bike without my jacket. Since I was just riding around town, and possibly to a restaurant, I had removed the jacket and left it in the room. When I tried to start the bike, I got an error message on the display to enter a PIN code for the security system. I did not have a PIN code for the security system, but I had the card that indicated where it could be written down.

I called the H.O.G. support number, but after a long while, they really did not have an answer. I also called Most Wanted Harley-Davidson®, even though it was after hours, to ask if there was a solution. Fortunately, I remembered I had the other fob in the room, so I went in and picked it up and came back with it and the bike started. The next morning, Most Wanted Harley-Davidson® called me back and we concluded the "failed" fob may just need a battery and they had several. I said I would be there and buy two of them. That was all it needed. Panic over.

Back to the evening after the panic was over, it was still sunny with the white clouds swirling about making it very pleasant. The ride around town had a settling effect after the earlier excitement and I got out on the highway a little bit. I wanted to come back into town a different direction, but I got behind a box – again. Stopping at an intersection back at Route 50, I observed a train on the track that parallels Route 50 and I then turned and went alongside the train for a little way back to the hotel. I parked the bike at the hotel and walked across the street to the Casa Alvarez and had a fine dinner. After a good meal I walked back across the street to Freddy's and got an ice cream cone. I enjoyed that as I walked back to the room and took care of things for the night. I believe I had a good night's sleep.

Leaving
Ottawa,
Kansas

Entering
Emporia,
Kansas

The
Warkentin
House

Kansas
Wheat
Fields

Kinsley,
Kansas

Finally
Gas at
Offere,
Kansas

Entering
Dodge
City,
Kansas

Most
Wanted
Harley-
Davidson®

The
Wyatt
Earp
Hotel

Long
Trains
and
Shadows

Day 8

Plan

Day	Starting Point / Ending Point	Miles / Ride Time	Potential Lodging	Potential Dining at Destination	Potential Attractions En Route
8 (Thu, July 16)	Dodge City, KS Salida, CO	384 7:14	Comfort Inn; Baymont; American Classic Inn; Salida Hotel; Circle R Hotel	The Lost Cajun; 50 Burger Shakes & Beer; Fiesta Mexicana Family Restaurant	• Breakfast at Miss Kitty's Café (Take-out); • Santa Fe Trail Tracks, West of Dodge City; • Welcome to Colorful Colorado Sign; • Lunch at Becky's Restaurant, Lamar, CO (Take-out); • Colorado Welcome Center, Lamar, CO; • Madonna of the Trail Monument, Lamar; • Gas up at Love's in Lamar; • Pueblo Weisbrod Aircraft Museum; • Outpost H-D, Pueblo, CO; • The Winery at Holy Cross Abbey, Canon City, CO • Royal Gorge Bridge and Park

Actual

Day	Starting Point / Ending Point	Miles / Ride Time	Lodging	Dining at Destination	Attractions En Route
8 (Thu, July 16)	Dodge City, KS Pueblo, CO	309 7:14	La Quinta Inn	Cracker Barrel;	• Breakfast at Dodge House (Dine-In); • Visitor Center; • Post Office; • Most Wanted H-D to get key FOB battery; • Santa Fe Trail Tracks, West of Dodge City (Rode through with dash cam on); • Gas up at Garden City, KS; • Lunch at Wagon Wheel, Lakin, KS (Dine-In); • Welcome to Colorful Colorado Sign; • Gas up at Love's in Las Animas, CO; • Outpost H-D, Pueblo, CO; • Cracker Barrel for supper (Dine-In)

Well, Thursday was following suit to alternative changes as Miss Kitty's was closed, so I went to the visitor's center. Clouds were starting to form, and I was not sure that I was going to get out of Dodge in time, but anyway I went over to the Visitor Center and talked with the ladies there. When I asked about postcards, they wanted to give me several hundred of them, because they were changing the motif from the "Get the Heck into Dodge" theme, so they were just giving them away. I got five each of four different types of cards and they recommended the Dodge House restaurant for breakfast. So that was where I went for breakfast. The rain passed through overnight, so looking to the West, everything was looking pretty clear by that time.

I knew they had a Daylight Donuts there in Dodge City and Daylight Donuts has probably my favorite donut, which is their old fashioned, a really good sour cream type of cake donut. It was a long line for the drive through and I was going to have a little difficulty doing that on the bike. The line came all the way out to the street, so I did not stay there, and I went out came back around later but they were all out of my favorites, so I had to settle for some alternatives for the donuts as well. I did get a couple of substitutes to try them later for a snack.

At the Boot Hill complex, they had a special steam engine on display, and I got a photo of that. While there, I observed the Dodge City Statuary and Boot Hill Museum. [40] [41] The next thing to see was the Santa Fe Railroad tracks and then the Colorado line. Leaving the little bit of rain that was starting to roll into Dodge City behind, I got out to the open highway and had blue skies and white wispy clouds in the sky. I went by the Santa Fe Trail tracks, but I really did not get off the bike because it was going to be a little bit of a problem parking, so I said I would just move along. I had taken time with going back to Most Wanted Harley-Davidson® to get the key fob battery and needed to make tracks for Colorado.

Because of the late start out of Dodge City, I could not make it in time to Becky's restaurant as planned, but I made it to the Wagon Wheel before they closed in Lakin, Kansas, which also was a Daylight Donuts, but I did not need any more that day. I did eat a good burger and onion rings which really hit the spot. The lady that owns the place also works at the courthouse and I met up with her daughter and son who were holding down the fort for the afternoon. The daughter, Bailey, was going into the sixth grade and she was running the store that day. Her younger brother, Reed, was also helping out. He was going into fifth grade for the first time and was apprehensive about middle school. We had a really nice visit as they came over and sat at the table where I was sitting. They were really nice kids.

That was the last stop before I crossed into Colorful Colorado as the welcome sign states and it was very much like Kansas at that point with long straight roads and flat areas. The clouds were starting to form and get a little dark, so I had to just see what was going to take place. It did not really rain much on me at that point. There were a couple of detours for US 50 around Rocky Ford, Colorado which took you out to the North, over to the West and back down to the South to get back to Route 50. But that also took me away from some of the storm activity. I did go through a bunch of wind, just straight wind from the south side. Anyway, I got back onto the true Route 50 and captured a photo of a train and the rain headed towards me. At least that is what it looked like. The train was definitely headed towards me, but I was not sure about the rain and I got into a little bit of rain that did not really get me wet.

Nearing Pueblo, Colorado, I noticed the ominous storm clouds in the distance, but they never did get me though, as I made it to Pueblo just in time. I made it to Outpost Harley-Davidson®, where I met up with Hannah, who helped me with a shirt and poker chips. I also gave her a Ride for Kids® card and she was interested in just making a donation. Her dad had a brain tumor, so she was a little sensitive when I mentioned the Pediatric Brain Tumor Foundation. I decided to stay in Pueblo overnight instead of going the other seventy-six miles to Salida because that is up in the mountains. I skirted around storms the whole way to Pueblo, it seemed, and the wind was very gusty at times, but not much of anything with respect to rain. It looked like the radar was saying over the mountains it was going to be nasty.

From Outpost Harley-Davidson®, I decided I would go up to the LaQuinta Inn, just up the street. You could see it from the shop, and they had rooms available, so I decided to stay there. Another biker came in from Denver through Grand Junction to Pueblo, and he said it rained all the way through. He said he was on some of those roads and only going 20 miles an hour and that type of thing. I was glad I did not just charge into that weather that night. I knew I would have some alternatives for stops along the way and may not get to the destinations designated in the plan, but, hey, that is what the plan is for. You have a plan and then you modify it according to your circumstances.

Dinner was at the Cracker Barrel, which was also within walking distance from the hotel.

Miss
Kitty's
Café
Was
Closed

Boot
Hill
Center
Before
Actually
Opening

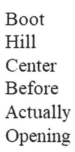

Boot
Hill
Special
Steam
Engine

Dodge
House
for
Breakfast

Getting
Out of
Dodge

Colorful
Colorado

Colorado
is a lot
like
Kansas
Here

Heading
Into the
Train
and the
Rain

Plan

Day	Starting Point / Ending Point	Miles / Ride Time	Potential Lodging	Potential Dining at Destination	Potential Attractions En Route
9 (Fri, July 17)	Salida, CO Green River, UT	394 7:38	Super 8; Comfort Inn; River Terrace; First Choice Inn	Tamarisk Restaurant; Ray's Tavern; Chow Hound; Tacos La Pasadita	• Breakfast at Patio Pancake Place (Dine-In);; • Monarch Pass Overlook; • Gunnison Pioneer Museum, Gunnison, CO; • Black Canyon of the Gunnison National Park, South Rim Visitor Center, Montrose; • Lunch at Crash Burger, Montrose, CO (Take-out); • Gas up in Montrose, CO; • View of Colorado National Monument to the South near Grand Junction, CO; • Gas up at Papa Joe's Stop & Go, Thompson Springs, UT; • Arches National Park (To Devil's Garden Trailhead), Moab, UT; • Old Highway 50 into Green River, UT;

Actual

Day	Starting Point / Ending Point	Miles / Ride Time	Lodging	Dining at Destination	Attractions En Route
9 (Fri, July 17)	Pueblo, CO Green River, UT	382 6:56 With no side trips	Motel 6	Tamarisk Restaurant	• Breakfast at Country Kitchen, Pueblo, CO (Dine-In); • Gas up in Pueblo, CO; • Holy Cross Monastery ride through with dash cam; • Royal Gorge Bridge and Park, Canon City, CO; • Lunch at the Lost Cajun, Salida, CO (Dine-In); • Gas up in Salida, CO; • Monarch Pass Overlook (Ride by with dash cam); • Grand Junction H-D; • Gas up in Grand Junction: • Old Highway 50 into Green River, UT; • Tamarisk Restaurant for supper (Dine-In)

Friday morning started off with an alternative. I had picked the Village Inn as my choice to have breakfast because they were going to be open at 6:00. I got there at six thirty and the sign says they did not open until 7:00. I wanted to head out early, so just down the street a little bit was the Country Kitchen. I had a garden vegetable omelet and pancakes and I got full. I did not eat all the hash browns either. Exceptionally good breakfast. A good breakfast was a good start for the day and after the rain that came through the night before was all gone, it was a bright sunny day. It was a much better day to head up into the mountains, but first, I was out there on this big plain area which was just a wide-open space and straight road. It was hard to believe that it was over 5000 feet elevation, but it certainly was on that part of US 50. As I headed out of Pueblo, I stopped to take a few photos along the way just to show that I was on the road with the mountains in the distance. Getting closer to the mountains, the road for a long way was just super straight, but I will take those as well as the twisties.

Then I rode into Cañon City, Colorado, home of the world-famous Royal Gorge Bridge & Park, Holy Cross Abbey, the Winery at Holy Cross Abbey, Royal Gorge Route Railroad line through Colorado's grandest canyon and many others. Cañon City was founded in 1860 to excavate possible mineral deposits in the area. [42]

I stopped into the Abbey, rode through the grounds and it is a genuinely nice campus. [43] Riding through downtown Cañon City takes you back to the Old West somewhat as many of the old buildings have been maintained with their ornate brickwork and architecture. [44]

Next on track was the ride to the Royal Gorge Bridge, which is an immensely popular scenic area. I was there before they actually opened up, but I did take a look around and took some pictures. It is an awesome site to see. I later learned more about the bridge, the gorge, and the railroad. [45]

I took a picture of me in front of the Rio Grande 499 steam engine that was there with the gorge, the bridge, and the mountain range in the background. When I left the bridge area, I got into the hills with a few twisties up there. US 50 parallels the Arkansas River for about 50 miles with the river on the right. It was an illusion because you knew that you were heading uphill, because the water was rushing toward you, but the sensation that you were going downhill was always there. It was amazing and just beautiful country through there with blue skies abounding at the time. The scenery in that area was just awesome, as always is the case with God's creation. [46]

Before getting to Salida, Colorado, there was an accident around the bend. We (me and the other folks stopped on the road) could not see where it was, but it had cars backed up for a good way down the road. We sat there and the police had come by and said, "it's going to be awhile" and so everybody was just parked on the road there with engines off and visiting in the hot sun. I got a couple of pictures of that area where we were stranded on the highway. I was stopped at about 10:30 local mountain time.

While I was parked there on the road, hearing the Arkansas River to the right of me down below reminded me of how weird it seemed like the road was going downhill, but the river keeps coming towards you, so it was flowing downhill against where I was going. So, I must have been going up, but I just always had that sensation of going downhill. The river was coming toward me, so it just seemed weird for about 50 miles, as the elevation climbed from 5331 feet to 7083 feet.

So, the accident put the kibosh on the original plan because it was just outside of Salida, and so I decided to go ahead and eat lunch in Salida at the Lost Cajun Restaurant. They have an excellent shrimp sandwich and the excellent waitress, Carrie made it a great experience. I gave her a card and I gassed up at the store right next door and headed out to see where I could go. They call Salida the "Gem of the Rockies" [47]

I got into higher elevations as I motored out of Salida and towards Gunnison. The clouds were white puffies with rich blue skies behind them. US 50 kept on rising to the higher elevations to what I refer to as the Alpine region and even up there I could not escape the road work and the construction signs. There is a wide spot in the Gunnison River where it is almost like a lake, but is still called the Gunnison River, so I stopped for a photo op. Some clouds started forming and I thought maybe it was going to be overcast as I got closer to Montrose, Colorado, and invariably, I was spit on a little bit.

In Grand Junction, Colorado, I finally made it to Grand Junction Harley-Davidson® and a nice young lady by the name of Natasha helped me with the poker chips and I gave her a card and she was going to share it. For my photo op there, I actually had a fella take it for me because I could not set up my selfie stick tripod to get it done due to the parking traffic. He got me the photo there and I was looking a mess because it was hot, and I had my helmet off, and I just had not cleaned up enough, but hey, it was a typical biker look.

Then I left Colorado and it was still cloudy, but blue skies and sunshine were still behind some of the clouds and I got some photos of that going into Utah. The Utah sun was setting as I reached Green River, Utah and I was able to find a good place to stay and a good place to eat. Fish tacos were on special that night at the Tamarisk Restaurant, and they were wonderful indeed.

Leaving
Pueblo,
Colorado

Selfie to
Prove I
Was
More
Than
Just a
Shadow

Cañon
City,
Colorado

Royal
Gorge
Bridge

Royal
Gorge
Railroad
Engine

Optical
Illusion –
The River
is Flowing
Toward Me

"Gem of the Rockies" – Salida, Colorado

Gunnison River

Grand
Junction
Harley-
Davidson®

Leaving
Colorful
Colorado

Entering
Utah

Entering
Green
River,
Utah

Day 10

Plan

Day	Starting Point / Ending Point	Miles / Ride Time	Potential Lodging	Potential Dining at Destination	Potential Attractions En Route
10 (Sat, July 18)	Green River, UT Ely, NV	352 5:57	Motel 6; Ramada; Bristlecone Motel; La Quinta Inn;	Jr. Street Tacos; Hunters; Hometown Pizza; Silver State Restaurant	• Breakfast at West Winds Restaurant (Dine-In); • CCC/POW Camp, Salina, UT (Open Sat 10-2); • Gas up in Salina (preventive); • Lunch at Zapata's, Delta, UT (Take-out); • May want to top off gas in Delta as preventive; • Gas up at Border gas station, Baker, NV (U.S. 50 Passport Stop); • Great Basin National Park, Baker, NV (would be worth a ride through); • Nevada Northern Railway Museum, Ely (U.S. 50 Passport Stop); • Mass at Sacred Heart (if before 1730)

Actual

Day	Starting Point / Ending Point	Miles / Ride Time	Lodging	Dining at Destination	Attractions En Route
10 (Sat, July 18)	Green River, UT Ely, NV	352 5:57	Motel 6	Hometown Pizza	• Post Office stop: • Breakfast at Melon Vine Food Store (Dine-In); • Gas up at Love's in Green River, UT; • Gas up in Salina (preventive); • Lunch at Zapata's, Delta, UT (Dine-In); • May want to top off gas in Delta as preventive; • Stop at Border gas station, Baker, NV (U.S. 50 Passport Stop); • Great Basin National Park, Baker, NV (was worth a ride through) • Hometown Pizza for supper (Take-out)

Breakfast for Day 10 was at Melon Vine Food Store in Green River, which is just a nice little grocery store that has a bakery on one end. I had some breakfast burritos, and they had some doughnuts and fritters, so I got one of each, a cup of coffee, and some water. Penny is the name of the cashier that helped me out and she is a genuinely nice lady.

Already in Utah, I headed out again with blue skies on a sunny day which felt like an exceptionally good day to ride. Utah, in my mind on this whole trip, probably had the most diverse landscape of any single state. It has your plains. It has your canyons. It has your red sandstone formations. It has deep canyons, valleys, farmland, and hills. You name it, it seems to have a little bit of that all along US 50 in Utah. God certainly displayed His multifaceted creativity in Utah.

I was just really enamored with the amount of diversity that Utah provides in its landscape, but I did find some boxes to follow in that beautiful landscape, as well. It was a good thing there were passing lanes in some of those areas, so I did not have to stay behind the box for very long.

Riding through Eagle Canyon then through Devils Canyon was really awesome and I was very appreciative that I was viewing it on my bike and not within the housing of a vehicle and that I was definitely not boxed in. The blue sky on that day was just awesome, it was such a deep shade of blue. As I got closer to Salina, Utah, there were some more mountains and mountain areas that I was able to see and the blue sky was still a tremendous deep color blue and some white puffs here and there. It was a great ride to get there with lots and lots of neat views that you probably cannot take or see from inside a can or "cage" (reference to cars and trucks). Of course, every state had to have road construction on the route that I take.

Eagle Canyon is located in the southern section of the San Rafael Swell west of Green River, Utah and the Devil's Canyon area is also remarkably interesting. [48]

There were a lot of picturesque areas near the Canyon Mountains and then it was wide open plains. After going through some of the canyon areas, the landscape just kept on changing the farther West I rode. As I motored toward Delta, Utah I could see the mountains in the distance because I was still on a big wide plain when that came into view. Then I started to see some clouds form, but blue eyes behind them remained a welcome backdrop.

I rode through Salina, Utah, but did not have time to stop to see the POW camp as I had planned because I really needed to get to Ely, Nevada before it was too late to get my US 50 passbook there. There is a little history about the area, and I found out more after the fact. [49] [50]

So, I got to Delta, Utah a little before 2:00 and found Zapata's Restaurant after getting some gas at the Shell station. Man, oh man, I got the Chili Rellenos, and it was a big plate. I could not eat everything, but I did eat the chilis but had to leave some of the rice and beans and chips and salsa. But anyway, after that great meal I rode off to head towards Ely, Nevada and Great Basin National Park and the Nevada Railway Museum.

Across the state line in Nevada, a stop at the Border Gas Station and Motel in Baker, Nevada was the first of many of the US 50 in Nevada Loneliest Road checkpoints. I picked up my passbook there and got it stamped for the first time and said, "now I was starting my Loneliest Road journey." From there it was on to the Great Basin National Park to see the sights there. As I arrived at the park visitor center, I met some bikers that were in the parking lot and my dash cam was left on inadvertently, so I got a picture of myself handing out a card to one of them. I was carrying several cards for the Ride for Kids® fundraising effort that I was trying to support during this journey, so I caught myself on camera. Not wanting to take up photo space in the book, I decided to leave that one out. Next was the fun twisty road that heads up to Wheeler Peak, which is a very tall 13,000-foot peak that you can view but you cannot ride on so you get to about 10,000 feet and you can see it from a viewing area.

Wheeler Peak is within the southern part of the Snake Range, a chain of peaks that trend North-South to reach an elevation of 13,065 feet at the peak. Near Wheeler Peak's summit is the southernmost permanent icefield in the United States.

I took a few pictures with the dash cam coming down to see the Great Basin and all the surrounding area and the blue skies and white puffies along the way made it very enjoyable. Heading West toward Ely, Nevada which was my destination for the day was enjoyable indeed.

Sacramento Pass (7,154 feet) on the way to Ely, Nevada [51] is where U.S. Route 50, the "Loneliest Highway in America", crosses the Snake Range.

After checking in to the Motel 6, I rode over to Hometown Pizza to pick up supper and headed back to the room to once again perform the ritual of eat, upload photos, charge all the electronic devices and get some sleep.

More Utah landscape diversity.

Devil's Canyon Area

Some
Welcome
Curves

How
Quickly
the
Landscape
Changes

Entering
Salina,
Utah

Round
Hill to
Noon
Rock
Peak

Wheeler Peak from US 50 near the Nevada State line

Nevada State Line

Border
Gas
Station
and
Motel
Baker,
Nevada

Beginning
the
Loneliest
Road

Wheeler
Peak
Viewed
From 10k
Foot
Elevation

Wheeler
Peak 13k
Foot
Elevation

Great
Basin
View

Entering
Ely,
Nevada

Day 11

Plan

Day	Starting Point / Ending Point	Miles / Ride Time	Potential Lodging	Potential Dining at Destination	Potential Attractions En Route
11 (Sun, July 19)	Ely, NV Carson City, NV	322 5:22	Rodeway Inn At Nevada State Capitol; Hardman House Hotel; Carson Tahoe Hotel	Midtown Café; Cafe at Adele's; Living the Good Life	• Breakfast at Silver State Restaurant (Take-out); • 09:30 Mass if not Sat. Mass; • Eureka County Opera House, Eureka, NV (U.S. 50 Passport Stop); • Gas up in Eureka, NV; • Austin Justice Court, Austin, NV (U.S. 50 Passport Stop); • Lunch at Toiyabe Cafe or Silver State (pizza), Austin, NV (Take-out); • Gas up in Austin; • Sand Springs Pony Express Station, Sand Mountain, NV; • Churchill County Museum, Fallon, NV (U.S. 50 Passport Stop); • Gas up in Fallon, NV; • Dayton Area Chamber of Commerce, Dayton, NV (U.S. 50 Passport Stop); • Carson City Visitor Center, Carson City, NV (U.S. 50 Passport Stop, if before 1600); • Battle Born H-D, Carson City, NV (if before 1700); • Mills Park (Photo op)

Actual

Day	Starting Point / Ending Point	Miles / Ride Time	Lodging	Dining at Destination	Attractions En Route
11 (Sun, July 19)	Ely, NV Carson City, NV	322 5:22	Motel 6	Ming's; Peg's	• Mass online – 0430 Knoxville Cathedral; • (Silver State Restaurant phone disconnected, but apparently Nardi's opened in same building); • Post Office Drop; • Breakfast at Nardi's Family Restaurant (Dine-In); • Nevada Northern Railway Museum, Ely • Nevada Northern Railway Museum, Ely (U.S. 50 Passport Stop); • Owl Club, Eureka, NV (U.S. 50 Passport Stop);

Day	Starting Point / Ending Point	Miles / Ride Time	Lodging	Dining at Destination	Attractions En Route
					• Gas up in Eureka, NV; • Trading Post in Austin, Austin, NV (U.S. 50 Passport Stop); • (Toiyabe Café looked closed and inaccessible due to construction, learned later permanently closed); • Gas up in Austin; • Sand Springs Pony Express Station, Sand Mountain, NV (did not stop); • Texaco, Fallon, NV (U.S. 50 Passport Stop); • Gas up at Texaco in Fallon, NV; • Lunch at Texaco in Fallon (Take-out); • Dayton Taphouse, Dayton, NV (U.S. 50 Passport Stop); • Battle Born H-D, Carson City, NV; • Ming's for supper (Dine-In)

Day 11 started out early with "going" to Mass at the Cathedral in Nashville, Tennessee at 4:30 a.m. because I just woke up and decided it would be best to do that. I had planned to go to the local church in Ely, Sacred Heart, but did not check out the night before to see if they were having masses at the same times as I had previously learned, so once again, online turned out to be the choice I made.

Once on the road again, the traveling started by riding over to the Nevada Northern Railway to get my passbook stamped there as it is one of the checkpoint stations in Ely. [52]

Riding into downtown Ely, Nevada I was searching for Nardi's Restaurant. I had wanted to go to the Silver State Restaurant, and had called them, but their number was disconnected. I then looked up a restaurant called Nardi's because it seemed like it would be a good breakfast spot. Following the GPS, I went by there a couple of times wondering where it was, and it turns out that the restaurant is at the same location of the Silver State Restaurant. The Silver State Restaurant sign was big as day out at the street, but the GPS said it was Nardi's. The marquee under the Silver State Restaurant said something about Nardi's delivers, so that was a little confusing. As it turns out, Nardi's bought the Silver State and they have their name painted on the window, but it was kind of in the inside knee of the building there and that morning, it was in the shade so you really could not see it from the street. Anyway, I did get there for breakfast and it was a great breakfast for sure. The folks there are really good servants and that was a very enjoyable experience.

Since I had been through a few little showers the last few days, I wanted to find a self-serve car wash to at least start out on a dry day with the bike at least a little bit shiny. Well, there was a self-service car wash there, so I took the bike in after a fella left in a truck because they had two bays, but only one worked. I did at least get most of the grime off, so at least first appearance is the bike has not been in a rainstorm, so that turned out to be good.

Riding farther into the downtown, I caught sight of all the old-style casinos and hotels, which was interesting to see. After downtown, it was time to head out and, again, a lot of these towns along US 50 are still an old western style of buildings and really intriguing the way they laid out the buildings. Of course, there you have casinos, so you cannot get away from that in Nevada. Heading up to the mountains, it was interesting to note that US 50 and railroad tracks are kind of parallel a lot of the way and there was a railroad that goes through some of the mountains next to where the road goes around them. US 50 and the railroad often follow similar routes. One particular section shown in one of the photos belongs to a now abandoned line. [53]

Much of US 50 in Nevada is also part of the old Lincoln Highway, which connected New York to San Francisco in its time, one of the first cross-country motor roads. [54]

Nevada also has High Plains like some of the other states so what I did to prepare for the High Plains and for the mountains and the higher elevations and the dryness and so forth was to buy Pedialyte packs to mix in with a 20-ounce water bottle. In my case, I put water in my Black Rifle Coffee mug that I got specifically for this trip because it fits in the holder that I have on the front of the saddlebag. Then I kept the Pedialyte packs in a zipper plastic bag I kept in the pouch on the saddlebag. The whole reason for doing that is to keep your electrolytes up so you do not get dehydrated and start fainting and all that kind of stuff that happens when people, like me for instance, come from the East Coast and are not used to the higher elevations that can give you that type of malady.

In this particular area West of Ely, you can begin to think that maybe this might be the loneliest road, but who knows? Whether it is or not, I had great riding weather with blue skies everywhere. I do not remember seeing a whole lot of clouds starting out, so it was just very pleasant as I headed toward Eureka, Nevada.

Before arriving in Eureka, I crossed the Pancake Summit, which is 6,517 feet in elevation and again, I was looking at some mountains in the periphery, but you know it was a straight flat area that I was riding through. It just boggles the mind that you are that high in elevation and Pinto Summit was another one at 7376 feet elevation. Again, it does not give you the impression that you are up that high in elevation. Going through the Windfall Canyon area where Windfall Gold Mine was established after gold was found in this area in 1909 made me take note to do a little research later. [55]

Silver was discovered in Eureka in 1864, which made it America's first important lead-silver discovery. Smelting was required to separate the silver from the lead and many of them were built around Eureka. The problem with smelting is it generates much smoke and slag. The smoke was so heavy at times that black clouds floated over the town, leaving soot and dirt everywhere. Eureka became to be known as the "Pittsburgh of the West." [56]

Downtown Eureka, Nevada with the Opera House on the right and the Court House on the left, both locations for the US 50 passbook stamps, once again took me back to the Old West with its architectural style. There was a sign in the Owl Club Bar and Steakhouse, where I had my US 50 passbook stamped, that read, "We do not have WIFI, Talk to each other, Pretend it's 1995". I got a kick out of that one.

The next scenic wonder was going through what they call the Hickison Petroglyph Recreation Area, and I did not go off the road to go through there to look at the petroglyphs up close, but these are incredibly old markings and carvings into the mountains. While in that region, there were other bikers on the road, so it is always good to see other bikers along the route. [57] [58]

White puffy clouds started to come into play, but blue skies still abound in this area as I got closer to a town called Austin, Nevada and rode through part of the Toiyabe National Forest. The Humboldt-Toiyabe National Forest is the largest national forest in the lower 48 states. It is located in Nevada and a small portion of eastern California and covers an enormous expanse of 6.3 million acres. The Austin Summit, elevation 7484 feet, does not look like you are that high, but everything is higher in this area, so what should I have expected?

Entering Austin, which is located on the western slopes of the Toiyabe Range at an elevation of 6,605 feet was remarkably interesting. Looking around as I was riding into Austin, the whole town had construction going on in the road as far as you could see. It was full of cones and potholes and trenches and barricades and everything going on in Austin made it hard to get around. I think, probably because of the construction as well as the COVID-19 scenario some of the establishments were closed. Actually, it seemed like a lot were closed. [59]

Lunch was planned to be at the Toiyabe Café, but it looked to be closed, maybe for good. I did stop at the Trading Post, which was a checkpoint for the loneliest road. There I met Julie Mills, the owner of the trading post and we had a nice conversation. I had my passbook stamped by her and I also purchased a US 50 patch and pin. Lunch this day was one of those get a sandwich at the gas station and stand by the bike type of fine dining, so after that I got back on the road heading West. Passing the Austin Cemetery seemed to be interesting and a little post trip research provided the rest of the story. [60]

The Mount Airy Summit – Elevation 6679 feet again it just does not look that high an elevation. Next one up was Drumm Summit – Elevation 4623 feet heading down now I guess and of course I found another box to get behind on this long straight road. I passed by the Salt Wells, also known as Eight Mile Flat, which is located near Fallon in Churchill County, Nevada. Lithium and boron are extracted from this area.

Entering Fallon, home of the annual Cantaloupe Festival and Churchill Country Fair, DeGolyer Bucking Horse and Bull Bash, Tractors and Truffles, World Cowboy Fast Draw Championship, No Hill Hundred Century Bicycle Tour, and other events. Fallon is called the "Oasis of Nevada."

Some key facts and historical notes:

Construction of the 36-mile-long Truckee Canal was begun in 1905;

Lahontan Dam was completed in 1914;

A national USRS advertising campaign brought homesteaders to the area;

Fallon was officially incorporated in 1908. [61]

In Fallon, I chose to just grab sandwiches and chips and stuff like that from the Texaco, which was also one of the stamp stations for US 50. I had already gassed up elsewhere, but I went there and sat out on the picnic table under a shelter and had a lunch. Because it was ridiculously hot then. That is where I got my stamp in Fallon.

In Dayton I got my passbook at the Dayton Tap House. Daisy and Wendy were so pleasant and accommodating and may actually put some things on social media because of the Ride for Kids®. At any rate, it was a great day, and the weather was fantastic.

I rolled into Carson City, Nevada, which was the last checkpoint of my US 50 loneliest ride and got into town just before the rain started as it was starting to cloud up as I got closer. I was able to get to Battle Born Harley-Davidson® for my poker chips, a shirt, and a Ride 365 photo op. After that, I had to pick up a 1 terabyte external hard drive at Walmart to move all my dash cam photos from the computer hard drive as I had almost filled it up by this point. In addition, I got into the hotel before it rained for a little bit and then I was able to just walk (because I did not want to get the bike wet and messy on the road) over to Ming's and had dinner.

Once again, I go through the nightly routine of transferring dash cam photos from the SD card to the, now expanded, computer hard drive to make room for the next day's photos.

The
Nevada
Northern
Railway
Complex

Ely,
Nevada

Silver
State is
now
Nardi's

Inside
Nardi's

Leaving Ely and What is Shown on Maps as an Abandoned Rail Line

Is this really the loneliest road?

Windfall
Canyon
Area

Downtown
Eureka,
Nevada

Hickison
Petroglyph
Recreation
Area

Hickison
Summit –
Elevation
6500 feet

Entering
Austin,
Nevada

Liking the
Austin
Landscape

The
Trading
Post

The
Austin
Cemetery

Old
Town
Fallon,
Nevada

Entering
Carson
City
Before
the Rain

Day 12

Plan

Day	Starting Point / Ending Point	Miles / Ride Time	Potential Lodging	Potential Dining at Destination	Potential Attractions En Route
12a (Mon, July 20)	Carson City, NV Sacramento, CA	131 2:41	N/A	N/A	• Breakfast at Betsy's Café (Take-out); • View of Lover's Leap south of Lake Tahoe; • Shingle Springs State Historic Landmark 456, Shingle Springs, CA; • Arco Station on 16th, Sacramento, CA (US 50 End) Photo op; • Gas up at Arco Station; • Lunch at Willie's Burgers, Sacramento, CA (Take-out); • Walk over to see Historical Tower Café
12b (Mon, July 20)	Sacramento, CA Clearlake, CA	105 2:06	Americas Best Value Inn & Suites - Clearlake/ Wine Country	Fosters Freeze	• H-D of Sacramento; • Hotel; • (Laundry Day - Village Laundromat) • Get Fosters Freeze Takeout

Actual

Day	Starting Point / Ending Point	Miles / Ride Time	Lodging	Dining at Destination	Attractions En Route
12 (Mon, July 20)	Carson City, NV Clearlake, CA	236 4:47	Americas Best Value Inn & Suites - Clearlake/ Wine Country	"Foods, Etc." grocery store for eat in room supper and breakfast	• Laundry at Laundromat, Carson City; • Post Office stop; • Breakfast at Peg's, Carson City, NV (Dine-In); • Carson City Chamber, Carson City, NV (U.S. 50 Passport Stop); • Mills Park (Photo op): • Too much traffic and not worth the effort to catch the planned stops in Sacramento for US 50 historical endpoint; • H-D of Sacramento; • Gas stop in Woodland, CA; • Snack at Woodland, CA; • Supper from Foods, Etc.

This day was also the beginning of the last leg of my US 50 trek because Sacramento was the western end point for US 50. Then I would move along the California roadways up to Clearlake, California, but starting off in Carson City, I did a few errands. It was Monday morning, and I woke up early and decided that, since I had time, I would go ahead and do laundry that morning and try to do it at the motel, but that did not open up until 8:00 and this was before 6:00. The lady there said that there was a laundromat that opened up at six o'clock. So, to the north end of town I went, did laundry and came back down to go to breakfast.

After I did laundry, I went to the post office and mailed some things home, which I did not receive until two months later, but that was OK, I guess. What was sent home was some extra shirts and the sort of things I did not need after purchasing other T-Shirts. I went to the Carson City Chamber of Commerce to get my passbook stamped there and then I had what turned out to be an exceptionally large breakfast at Peg's Glorified Ham n Eggs. I had one of her famous skillets served by a nice young lady by the name of Dale D. She did really well, so I left her a card for the Ride for Kids®. A great way to start the day in Carson City is a great breakfast at Peg's Glorified Ham n Eggs.

After that great breakfast I then came back to the motel to rearrange clothes and set up for the next few days. So that was what I was doing when my youngest daughter, Sarah called me. I had texted her earlier asking if we could do a Google Duo sometime to see the grandkids. Then lo and behold, she joined up and called me, so I got to see them and talk with her and the kids and see the babies on the monitor because they were sleeping. (She has a 6-year-old daughter and two sets of boy/girl twins ages 4 years and 7 months at that time). Then, it was time to get all of the things organized and then get my shower and get out of there.

Traveling through Carson City the day after the rain with everything still under construction it reminded me of how Austin was since there were cones everywhere and roads were torn up. There were big holes, big excavations and it seemed like the whole city was just really a construction zone. Annabelle and I managed to get through it and rolled into downtown and saw the many casinos there in downtown Carson City.

Carson City, Nevada is named for the famous frontiersman and scout Christopher "Kit" Carson. John C. Fremont had named Carson City's nearby river for Kit Carson who was Fremont's scout during their 1843-1844 expedition. Carson City was founded as a community in 1858, seven years after the first settlement of Eagle Station trading post in 1851. [62]

Who would have thought that there is a Mills Park in Carson City? Mills Park is a large, multi-use, 51-acre community park that was made possible in large part by Edith Naomi Bremenkampf, who was appointed to a five-member committee by the mayor Caro Pendergraft of Carson in 1949 to examine possible sites to establish Carson City's first municipal park. She wrote about it in 1995 and described the sequence of events. [63] [64]

While trying to find my way through more construction to get to the road to get out of town I saw the mountains out there which were spectacular once again. This day was a pleasant sunny day with some white puffy clouds but for the most part it was very sunshiny. The road kept getting higher and higher in elevation and I saw more of the alpine scenario as we (Annabelle and me) climbed higher and higher on US 50. The Carson Range of the Sierra Nevadas was another very scenic area that was very exhilarating to navigate on two wheels. [65]

Heading towards Lake Tahoe, the scenery was wonderful with views of the mountains while also climbing the mountains along with blue skies and white puffy clouds. The alpine area was certainly evident with the many trees as you approach the lake area including White Fir, Sugar Pine, Ponderosa Pine among the many that grow there.

And Lake Tahoe came into view, North America's largest mountain lake at an elevation of 6224 feet. It was most definitely beautiful.

Facts of Interest [66]

- One inch of Lake Tahoe equals about 3.33 billion gallons of water.
- Deepest Point in Lake Tahoe is 1,645 ft. in Crystal Bay, NV. The Empire State Building would not break the surface.
- About 2.7 million people per year come to Lake Tahoe.
- Some say a prehistoric creature like Scotland's Nessie lives in the lake. Most recent sighting: 1972.
- Of the six common Tahoe pines, the Sugar Pine is the tallest, up to 200 feet.
- The Peregrine Falcon, also the fastest animal on earth, has been clocked at 200 mph in the Lake Tahoe area.

Moving into California around the Lake Tahoe area I got another glimpse of the Lake with the trees around and then clouds started to come through and clouded things up a little bit. Still seeing the blue skies in the background, it started to look like it was getting a little more moisture up there, but still, it was a good view from the mountain down into the valley. Continuing down the mountain, I went through a little town. I guess maybe it was just a community, maybe it is just a four-inch town that has a sign in both sides of a 4x4, I do not know but the community of Strawberry was an enigma to see.

When I motored into Sacramento, the clouds had dissipated for the most part and it was just kind of a hazy blue sky. In the Sacramento area US 50 is on Interstate 80 and it was just a big freeway which I tend to try to avoid but I could not do so this time. I was having to ride the road and get there, so I did ride past the endpoint for US 50, made a U-turn there and came back to get the picture of the sign that said that Ocean City, Maryland was 3073 miles away.

It was good I made it to Harley-Davidson® of Sacramento and to talk to some really helpful folks there. It was so nice to pick up my poker chips from Amber, a sweet young lady, and do my Ride 365 photo op. I gave her a card as well and told her about the Ride for Kids® story. Saul also gave me a complimentary key chain fob and a bottle of water, which I gratefully accepted. From there, it was up to Clearlake, California, where I had a peaceful night on the lake shore. The area between Sacramento and Clearlake was involved in the Sonoma-Lake-Napa (LNU) fire later in the summer after I returned home. That was interesting, alarming really, to see that there was now a burning fire where I was on the road just weeks before.

Of course, I could not get away from the construction as I got closer to Clearlake. I had a surprisingly good spot after I had made reservations at this location, the Americas Best Value Inn Clearlake. It was just a standard motel location, but it was on the lake and had some pretty scenic views there.

Well, I fantasized about having a nice big steak for a celebration for completing US 50, but there was nothing to be found in Clearlake of that order. Taco Bell was open, but their computers were down, so they could not even do any orders or anything for me. So, then I went to the food store, "Foods, Etc." to get a beer and some snacks I guess, to have with tacos, if I could get some. Going back to Taco Bell did not change anything as they were still inoperable. Back to the food store, looked at stuff that could be microwavable and got something that would work for breakfast as well (Hot Pockets) for the morning. When checking out for the second time, the girl at the counter said, "Hey, you know, over in the deli, they discount leftover meals and that type of thing". So, I went over there and got me a Chicken Fettuccini dinner, which was good stuff, with broccoli and carrots, cauliflower, and garlic bread. The nice young lady cashier at "Foods, etc" was Sarah. She was genuinely helpful, extremely helpful, and we discussed motorcycles, Ride for Kids® and my ride across the country.

Back at the motel, I enjoyed my grocery store dinner, did my normal photo transfer routine and voice recording notes to be able to remember what I needed to put in this book. It was a good ending for a great riding day.

Great
Breakfast
at Peg's
Glorified
Ham n
Eggs

Downtown
Carson
City,
Nevada

Selfie at Mills Park in Carson City

The Carson Range of the Sierra Nevadas

And
Lake
Tahoe
came
into
view

Another
glimpse
of the
lake

I like the
views
coming
down the
mountain

Made the
180 for
the sign
for Ocean
City,
Maryland
3073
miles
away

Harley-Davidson® of Sacramento

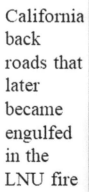

California back roads that later became engulfed in the LNU fire

Nearing
Clearlake,
California

My spot
for the
night in
Clearlake

Day 13

Plan

Day	Starting Point / Ending Point	Miles / Ride Time	Potential Lodging	Potential Dining at Destination	Potential Attractions En Route
13 (Tue, July 21)	Clearlake, CA Crescent City, CA	294 5:34	Motel 6 Crescent City; Quality Inn; Ocean View Inn; Travelodge; Bayview Inn;	Crescent City Crab Shack; SeaQuake Brewing; Chart Room; Fisherman's; Cristina's; The Good Harvest Café (Breakfast)	• Breakfast at hotel (ABV Inn); • Ridgewood Summit, Ridge, CA; • Drive-Thru Tree Park, Leggett, CA; • Lunch at The Peg House, Leggett, CA (Take-out); • Gas up in Leggett; • Immortal Tree, Redcrest, CA; • Redwood H-D, Eureka, CA; • Gas up in Eureka; • Redwood National Park - Kuechel Visitor Center; • Battery Point Lighthouse and Museum/Crescent City Lighthouse

Actual

Day	Starting Point / Ending Point	Miles / Ride Time	Lodging	Dining at Destination	Attractions En Route
13 (Tue, July 21)	Clearlake, CA Coos Bay, OR	294 5:34	Super 8	Dave's Pizza; SharkBite's Seafood Café;	• Breakfast at hotel (ABV Inn) (Hot Pockets); • Gas up in Clearlake, CA; • Ridgewood Summit, Ridge, CA (Drove over it, maybe dash cam?); • Drive through Tree Park (No way I was taking the bike down that "road"); • Lunch at The Peg House, Leggett, CA (Dine-out); • Gas up in Rio Dell, CA; • Redwood H-D, Eureka, CA; • Redwood National Park - Kuechel Visitor Center; • Gas up in Brookings, OR; • Supper at Dave's Pizza (Dine-In)

Well, it was Tuesday, and for starters, the package I was expecting never made it to the hotel yesterday, so I told the manager there that he had permission to open the package. They were Ride for Kids® cards and I asked him to hand them out to bikers or whoever else that he thought might be interested, so that was what he was going to do. After checking out, I went by the Foods, Etc, dropped off one of the do rags I had made for the trip for Sarah, gave it to Dawn, who was going to put it in the office for when Sarah came in to work. It was then time to head off to Coos Bay, Oregon.

God started me out again with another beautiful sunny day and I took a few pictures of the Lake from the hotel balcony, which was very peaceful. Heading out on California 20 to get up to US 101, it was a clear bright sun, blue sky morning, which was going to be my northerly route to get to the US 20 endpoint up there in Newport, Oregon. Of course, I ran into construction signs again along the way and then joined up with US 101 south of Willits, California. Riding by the 1,953-foot Ridgewood Summit, which is supposed to be the highest point for US 101, was remarkably interesting to note.

One of the destinations that I had put on my "potential attractions" along the route was the Drive Through Tree Park, near Leggett, which is supposed to be an interesting thing to go do. There had been rain in the days prior to me getting there, so things were kind of wet, especially since the tree canopy kept the sun from hitting much of the road surface. When I got go to the entrance where the sign was, it was kind of gravel and dirt and muddy and the road down to the tree was going to be a real pain and I just could not see any farther as the drive went downhill. It did not look too inviting for motorcycles, so I said I would forego the Drive Through Tree this trip. I just did not know what I was going to get into down there, so I moved on. I had to get back up to Highway 101 and the redwoods were starting to really come into play a lot and this section of Highway 101 is appropriately called the Redwood Highway.

I planned to stop for lunch in Leggett, California, but in the little town, I could not see much in the way of restaurants. Heading farther North on US 101, I found the Peg House Grill near Leggett, California, which had been the planned stop from the start, but I was looking for it in the town of Leggett. The lunch was a great experience at the Peg House Grill. I had to eat outside, but that was just how they do it all the time, not just for COVID-19. It is the type of place where you go to window, get your burger order in, and then pick it up when they call your name, all open air. They have picnic tables set up and it is just a nice place to eat. Even though it was like 10:45, I found myself having lunch, chowing down on their Lost Burger (or something like that) with goat cheese and lettuce, onions, avocado, which was good stuff. So, it was a pretty neat little spot to stop.

Redwood Harley-Davidson® was next on the Highway 101 journey, in the Eureka area, and I picked out my poker chips and took a photo op out front. Rolling right along up the highway and seeing all the redwoods was really awesome and then came the fog from the ocean, even before I got to Oregon. I did stop at Redwood National Park at the Kuechel Visitor Center near Orick, California and picked up a patch and a few post cards. [67]

There are a whole lot of redwoods all along US 101, some of which are right on the side of the road where the road makes a curve and the tree is right there in the curve, so I was going around the trees, basically. I got back out to the ocean view and the fog was out there with the ocean, but I saw some blue sky and white wispies over the land. I made it to Crescent City, California, the last California city there before crossing over to the Oregon Coast. [68]

Crescent City has endured gold mining, logging, and a horrific tsunami that hit the town in 1964 and still survives today as a tourist attraction. One point of interest (which was so popular that I could not find a safe place to park the bike along the twisty road) is the Battery Point Lighthouse, where keepers have resided there since 1856. [69]

When I got to the Oregon side of things and the "Oregon Coast" as they call it, famous for "Riding the Oregon Coast", I almost missed seeing the Oregon state line sign because it was partially behind a box, that was parked on the side of road. Again, my term for trucks or RV's is a "box." First look at the Oregon Coast was near the Pistol River area where there was a real conflict way back in 1856. [70]

The fog had mostly lifted as I rolled into Gold Beach, Oregon and the Gold Beach area was quite interesting. [71] The Isaac Lee Patterson bridge across the Rogue River right there in Gold Beach is one of many designed by Conde B. McCullough, the first of several I would cross riding up Highway 101. [72]

One thing I found interesting were the beaches of Oregon and in 1967 the Oregon Beach Bill made the entire coastline open to the public. Somewhere along this coast was Battle Rock, the site of the wreck of the Cottoneva in 1937. [73]

Well, I made it to Coos Bay before any kind of really bad weather came through, even though there was some fog and a little misty rain. I was able to get to the hotel where I was going to stay the night without much dampness. It certainly was windy to get here on the Oregon Coast, but it was kind of awesome to see the waves and so forth crashing on to the big rocks along the way. I walked a few blocks to get to Dave's Pizza, which was excellent. I talked with Melanie there and she is one of the do it all, you know, wait staff, cook staff, clean up staff type of employee. She is one of those that does it all, but I think they all do there. I gave her a Ride for Kids® card just so that she could share it at the restaurant. I then walked back to the hotel for the nightly routine and some sleep. The next day was going to be service day for Annabelle, my motorcycle, at Highway 101 Harley-Davidson®.

Morning
view
from my
motel
balcony

Rounding
Clearlake

Joining
Highway
101

Ridgewood
Summit

The
Name is
right for
Highway
101 in
California

On the
coast
came the
fog

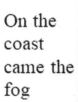

Into the
northern
California
redwoods
again

Return
of the
ocean
and
the fog

Entering
Crescent
City,
California

Bring
on the
Oregon
Coast

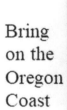

The
Oregon
State
Line

First
look at
the
Oregon
Coast

Gold
Beach,
Oregon

The
Isaac
Lee
Patterson
Bridge

A View
of the
Oregon
Coast

Somewhere
along this
coast was
Battle Rock

Day 14

Plan

Day	Starting Point / Ending Point	Miles / Ride Time	Potential Lodging	Potential Dining at Destination	Potential Attractions En Route
14 (Wed, July 22)	Crescent City, CA Lebanon, OR	308 6:42	Valley Inn Motel; Cascades City Center Motel; Shanico Inn; Best Western Premier Boulder Falls Inn;	Kevin's Café; The Lobby; James Gang Pizza; Bigfoot Bites; Sugar Vibes	• Breakfast at Apple Peddler (Take-out); • Highway 101 H-D, Coos Bay, OR; • Lunch at Blue Heron Bistro (German), Coos Bay, OR (Dine-In); • Gas up in Coos Bay; • Heceta Head Lighthouse, Florence, OR; • Thor's Well, Yachats, OR; • Walgreen's Parking Lot, Newport, OR (Start of US 20); • Gas up in Newport

Actual

Day	Starting Point / Ending Point	Miles / Ride Time	Lodging	Dining at Destination	Attractions En Route
14 (Wed, July 22)	Coos Bay, OR Lebanon, OR	165 3:26	Cascades City Center Motel	Kevin's Café; Wing Ming Restaurant	• Breakfast at Mom's Kitchen, Coos Bay, OR (Dine-In); • 20k Service for Annabelle (My bike) at Highway 101 H-D, Coos Bay, OR; • Lunch at Shark Bites, Coos Bay, OR (Dine-In) (Blue Heron not open for lunch); • Gas up in Reedsport, OR; • (Too windy and traffic was chaos for planned stops); • Walgreen's Parking Lot, Newport, OR (Start of US 20); • Supper from Wing Ming Restaurant in motel (Take out)

I think I slept pretty well that night in Coos Bay and kind of woke up on my own at four something and laid around until five something. It was almost six when I decided to roll out of bed, but I was trying to catch up from, you know, postcards and all the different files that I was trying to save, so anyway, the day was going to be servicing Annabelle, at Highway 101 Harley Davidson®. After having a great breakfast at Mom's

Kitchen, I emptied my saddlebags and then made my way back to Highway 101 Harley-Davidson® where I had scheduled to have Annabelle in for her 20,000-mile service. I spent the wait time picking out poker chips and a shirt, after which, I was able to get another photo op. After that, I had lunch at Shark Bites Café, a great lunch spot, and then packed up at the motel.

When it came time to leave, I left out of there and rode by some of the commercial fishery equipment that was up on the right-hand side of the road heading North because it is part of that Bay area. Just past that scene, I see a tsunami hazard zone, oh boy! I had seen a number of them along Highway 101, so I did a little more research and found out that in 1964 the largest earthquake in US history started up in Alaska. It created a tsunami that went a long way down the coast and killed over 100 people in three different states, so it was pretty massive.

The same tsunami that I mentioned when sharing about Crescent City, California was considered the most destructive tsunami to hit the United States. On March 27, 1964, the largest earthquake in US history originated in Prince William Sound just outside Anchorage, Alaska. The waves of the tsunami rolled over the west coast, from British Columbia to California and killed more than 100 people in Alaska, Oregon, and Crescent City, California. [74] After that signage I crossed the Conde B. McCullough Memorial Bridge across the Coos Bay and the North Bend Lower Range Channel. [75]

After leaving Coos Bay, riding up the coast on US 101 to Newport, Oregon, it was very windy and somewhat chilly, but not as cool as the day before. It was definitely windy, so that was a challenge getting up there, because every time I just headed north, I had the hill or the mountain to the right of me most of the time, so when I made right turns, I was coming around the corner and then the wind gusts just hit me. You just do not know which way you were going to get blown, so you must really take it cautiously, more so than normal. But anyway, that was still a fun challenge.

The Umpqua Lighthouse scenic viewpoint was interesting, but I could not really see too much as there was still some fog out there over the water and rolling onto the land. [76]

Entering Reedsport and then crossing the Umpqua River Bridge was fascinating. It was built across the second largest river between the Sacramento and the Columbia Rivers and designed by Conde B. McCullough (1887-1946), who was responsible for the design of at least five major bridges along the Oregon Coast Highway, and I rode across all five. [77]

Crossing many of the bridges that Conde B. McCullough had designed and had built was remarkably interesting as the designs all had some ornate type of structure associated with it, not just functional structure. They all had some aesthetic value as well. One such bridge is the Siuslaw River Bridge, which crosses the Siuslaw River in Florence, Oregon. [78]

While I was riding up the Oregon Coast Highway [79], it really became very windy, not only this day but the day before, and the wind was just howling in from the coast. You must be careful, especially on a motorcycle, to not go so fast (I do not go fast around blind curves anyway) but that is another reason to be cautious because the wind could knock you around.

Continuing northward from Florence, I went by the Sea Lions Cave area [80], which was interesting, but I was not close enough to hear them if they were being vocal. I had planned a stop in Yachats, but the time and the wind just did not want to cooperate. [81]

Just before rolling into Newport, Oregon I crossed the Yaquina Bay Bridge, another of the works of Conde McCullough.

Newport is the western terminus of US 20 there at US Highway 101, so of course I get my photo op in for seeing the sign that tells you to Boston is 3365 miles to the East. Then heading away from the coast on US 20 and getting out of the wind I get across the Caughran Hill Summit, elevation 496 feet. The landscape just significantly changed as it became pine trees and other trees and so forth and no coast with the sun to my back as it got later in the day.

Riding into Corvallis, where the Oregon State University is located, and the signage for US 20 just is not all that great to tell you which road is US 20 once you get into town. That is typical, as I have found, so even when you are on the right road going out of town, it is one, two, three miles sometimes before you even see a sign and that was not even a sign on the road. It is a sign for the road that comes intersecting US 20 and it said "US 20" both ways. So that was the only way I knew I was on the right road.

As I headed towards Lebanon, Oregon, which was the destination for the night, and I went through the landscape and farmland and wide-open spaces, I could not help but be in awe of God's creation. Lebanon was founded by American wagon train pioneers searching for a place to put down roots and build up farms. [82] [83]

I was staying at the Cascade City Center Motel, you know, just an old school kind of place with all rooms on ground level in several buildings with exterior access doors. Dinner was collected by a walk over to Wing Ming Restaurant and I talked with Kristi while there. Kristi was interested in the Ride for Kids®, so I gave her a card and she said she would look it up and share it with her motorcycle buddies. She said she and her husband used to ride when he had a bike. But anyway, I found myself sitting down in the room because it was take-out only over there at Wing Ming, so I said to myself, "I'll eat dinner." It was an incredibly good dinner at that.

After dinner was the nightly routine of digital transfer of information and recharging.

Highway
101
Harley-
Davidson®
After
Service

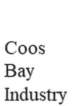

Coos
Bay
Industry

Tsunami
Hazard
Zone?

Conde B.
McCullough
Memorial
Bridge

Umpqua
River
Bridge

Siuslaw
River
Bridge

The
Oregon
Coast
Highway

Sea
Lions
Cave
Area

Yaquina Bay Bridge

Sign indicating the longest US highway in the country

Eastward
Bound

Downtown
Lebanon,
Oregon

Day 15

Plan

Day	Starting Point / Ending Point	Miles / Ride Time	Potential Lodging	Potential Dining at Destination	Potential Attractions En Route
15 (Thur, July 23)	Lebanon, OR Caldwell, ID	400 7:09	La Quinta Inn by Wyndham Caldwell	Mr. V's Family Restaurant (Dine-In); La Cocina (Dine-In);	• Breakfast at Kevin's Café (Cash Only), Lebanon, OR (Take-out); • Wildhorse H-D, Bend, OR; • Newberry National Volcanic Monument - Deschutes NF, Bend, OR; • Gas up in Bend; • Lunch at Taste of the Ranch, Brothers, OR (Take-out); • Gas stop in Hines, OR

Actual

Day	Starting Point / Ending Point	Miles / Ride Time	Lodging	Dining at Destination	Attractions En Route
15 (Thur, July 23)	Lebanon, OR Caldwell, ID	400 7:09	La Quinta Inn by Wyndham Caldwell	Burger King Restaurant (Dine-In) (Walking from Hotel)	• Breakfast at Kevin's Café (Cash Only), Lebanon, OR (Dine-In); • Gas up in Lebanon, OR; • Foster Reservoir; • Three Sisters Viewpoint; • Wildhorse H-D, Bend, OR; • Gas up in Bend, OR; • Lunch at Bogey's Burgers, Bend, OR (Dine-In); • Gas stop in Harper, OR (Should have gassed up before this stretch); • Supper at Burger King (Dine-In)

On Thursday morning, according to plan, I had breakfast at Kevin's Café and had the western scramble, which was excellent. I checked out of the Cascades City Center Motel and headed out to the East to Bend, Oregon.

Heading out from Lebanon, a little cluster of clouds dotted the blue sky, but it was not bad at all for riding. The first scenic view stop was the Foster Reservoir, a pretty, serene little reservoir. [84]

Riding along the tree lined road again in Oregon, I meandered through some curves and mountains and then the clouds broke up a little and blue skies and white puffies appeared. It is awesome to see with all the trees and the mountains and the roadways that have a little bit of a twist and turn.

Continuing eastward I passed the Hoodoo Ski Area and the Black Butte and then motored into Sisters,

Oregon, a quaint little town. Heading East out of Sisters, you never really get to see back over to the right, or the South, because of the trees mostly. There are three huge mountains there, but I did not realize that I could see them until I got down the road a bit and looked over my shoulder. By that time, I was out of the trees and it was wide open spaces on both sides of the road. The Three Sisters mountains that are still snow covered in July were right there in the now wide-open space after exiting the trees, so I did finally get to the viewpoint to see them. Then I stopped and looked at the mountains and took some pictures. It was awesome and that was absolutely amazing, and I may never have seen it had I not looked over my right shoulder because it really does not come into view heading East on US 20. It was a magnificently awesome sight to see, indeed.

Marker for the Sisters reads:

"This view of the Three Sisters and their neighbors to the north and south are mentioned in some of Oregon's earliest recorded history.

Many Explorers passed this way during the early 1800s.

Peter Skene Ogden, Hudson Bay Company trader and explorer, encountered this view in December of 1825.

Botanist David Douglas followed in October of 1826.

John C. Fremont was nearby in December of 1843, following ancient Indian trails in his southward exploration into Nevada and California.

Lieutenant H.L. Abbot of the Pacific Railroad Surveys wrote of this view of the Three Sisters in his journal on September 4, 1855: "This morning, after riding a few miles, we emerged from the forest, and traversed an elevated plateau, dotted with cedars [junipers] and sage bushes... The air was uncommonly clear and pure....The snowy peaks of the Three Sisters appeared quite near."

It is not known who first used the name Three Sisters to describe these peaks. In the early days, they were often referred to as Faith, Hope, and Charity, starting from the north. These names, however, did not prevail." [85]

Then, heading further East towards Bend, Oregon, the Maury Mountains came into view in the distance, and I experienced the wonder of the Creation once again viewing the beautiful landscape. Riding into Bend, Oregon, I stopped at Wild Horse Harley-Davidson®, got a shirt and poker chips and the young lady that helped me there was Shadow. We had a nice long discussion about horses, and she mentioned her husband was working in South Carolina and that she was going to go there and then leave the day I would return to Augusta. It is indeed a small world after all. But anyway, I gave her a Ride for Kids® card and she was really keen on it. She mentioned that she lost a 14-year-old sister to a brain tumor. So anyway, she was genuinely pleasant and personable. I was also able to get my Ride 365 photo op out front. For lunch, I had a great burger at Bogey's Burgers before leaving Bend, so Thursday was an alternative lunch location.

Motoring out of Bend, before reaching Burns, Oregon, I could see what I believed to be Wagontire

Mountain, which was beautiful. The wide-open space between me and the mountain along with the blue sky and white clouds made it very picturesque. It is always good to see another biker on the highway in those wide-open spaces in Oregon, and, for that matter, anywhere, and that afternoon, I did.

One thing that was really good out in those wide-open spaces was that there are rest areas in many locations, so I stopped in at the Sage Hen Rest Area Near Burns, Oregon and came out and continued heading East. The clouds were starting to thicken and get a little dark bottom, but I did not really get into anything weather wise that had any major consequences.

As I was heading out from Burns, I rode through Buchanan and then over the Stinkingwater Pass and the South Beede and North Beede reservoirs. Then, I noticed a sign that said no gas station for 68 miles, so I looked at the gas gauge and thought, "I have enough for 68 miles" and continued riding. Riding through the curves in the mountains, I was able to see the creeks and hills that flanked US 20, which just made for some awesome scenery. As I meandered through the rolling landscape, I kept an eye on the plummeting gas gauge and began to wonder if I had made the right decision to continue. Harper is the place that I stopped for gas at a little station there named Coleman's. If you go west on US 20, it will be 68 miles before you get to any other gas. And so, the sign was the same way coming east. And that was the station, a little old station that the owner named "Malfunction Junction" years back. I told him about the same title for the I-20 and I-26 interchange in Columbia, South Carolina. He thought that was really funny. His nickname for his junction was because it almost seemed like nothing worked there, you know, cell phones did not work and other things did not work, so he named it appropriately.

At first, I passed by, but it was a good thing I did stop there because Vale was a little bit farther than the gas, I probably had in the tank would have taken me. Maybe I could have made it to Vale, but it was one of those things you do not know, and you cannot get internet service on the cell phone, so you are kind of in the middle of nowhere. So, prudence says, go back and get gas. So that is what I did, and it was a pleasant stop. It is a down home place, with lots of folks sitting around inside jawing about the day and having a great time. It was just a really nice setup. The owner told me that the pump was terribly slow, but I said, "that was OK." He was not wrong about the pump, because it was a terribly slow pump for gas and it took me quite a while just to put 5 gallons in my 5-gallon tank, but it was no big deal, in reality.

Then I went through Vale, Oregon which had some neat buildings there and some very well painted murals on some of the buildings which were very well done. Another biker was headed the opposite direction and it is always good to get a wave from another friend I did not meet. [86] [87]

I passed a sign on a barn that said this is "Onion Country" so it might be for Oregon, but they are not Vidalias, that is for sure. Vidalia onions come from a select few counties in Georgia and are so good and sweet you can eat them like an apple, if you like onions. [88] Then it looked like in the distance after passing through that area, clouds started to become threatening, but it did not really seem to do anything.

Nyssa, Oregon, which is on the far east side of Oregon and pretty much last part of US 20 in Oregon, was part of the original plan as an overnight stop. I decided to change that as there were limited lodging choices and with the COVID-19 situation, I figured I should go a little farther East. [89]

After riding through Nyssa, I rode into Idaho and the weather began to look a little iffy up ahead. But then, the weather was simply great all day until I got closer to Caldwell, Idaho, about five miles out. It looked like it was really threatening and spinning and windy and so forth. I had already tucked my socks down in my boots so that they would not touch my pants legs in case we got wet because I was not going to put rain gear on for that a little bit. The pants were going to get washed some other time anyway, and I was not going wear them again the next day, so it did not matter. I was in and out of threatening clouds, but I did not really get wet anywhere and I got to my destination of Caldwell Idaho for the night. There was a little bit of rain in the area but most of it passed overnight and at this point I was not going to take the bike anywhere out in the rain again. I just walked over to the Burger King and had dinner and came back to the motel and took care of all my photos that take a while to transfer nightly to the hard drive.

Foster
Reservoir
Viewpoint

Foster
Reservoir

Oregon
Curves

Distant
Mountains

Sisters,
Oregon

Three
Sisters

Murals
in Vale,
Oregon

Onion
Country
but not
Vidalia

Nyssa,
Oregon

US 20
Into
Idaho

Day 16

Plan

Day	Starting Point / Ending Point	Miles / Ride Time	Potential Lodging	Potential Dining at Destination	Potential Attractions En Route
16 (Fri, July 24)	Caldwell, ID Ashton, ID	332 5:29	Eagle Peak Lodge	Big Jud's Ashton; Trails Inn Restaurant; Frostop Drive In;	• Breakfast at Sunrise Family Restaurant (Take-out); • Lunch at The Wrangler, Fairfield, ID (after 1100) (Take-out); • Gas up in Fairfield; • Craters of the Moon National Monument, Robert Limbert Visitor Center; • Experimental Breeder Reactor I, Arco, ID; • Grand Teton H-D, Idaho Falls, ID; • Gas up in Idaho Falls

Actual

Day	Starting Point / Ending Point	Miles / Ride Time	Lodging	Dining at Destination	Attractions En Route
16 (Fri, July 24)	Caldwell, ID Ashton, ID	332 5:29	Eagle Peak Lodge	Trails Inn Restaurant;	• Breakfast at Sunrise Family Restaurant (Dine-In); • Lunch at The Wrangler, Fairfield, ID (Dine-out); • Gas up in Silver Creek Store Texaco; • Craters of the Moon National Monument, Robert Limbert Visitor Center (Rode through the loop road in the park); • Experimental Breeder Reactor I, Arco, ID; (Closed) • Grand Teton H-D, Idaho Falls, ID; (Photo Op only) • Laundry down the street next to Trails Inn; • Supper at Trails Inn Restaurant (Dine-In)

Breakfast at the Sunrise Family Restaurant in Caldwell was excellent. Ashley B was my server and served me very well. Ashley B and the food were particularly excellent, and I thoroughly enjoyed it.

Day 16 was another beautiful morning, and the sun was up, with just some wispy clouds in the area, but it was just a very sunny day. Of course, heading East I was heading into the sun so that is always a challenge, but at least I was not really staring into the sun because it ended up being high enough above the horizon that it was not directly in my eyes. So, looking towards Boise, I motored along the highway.

Riding into Boise, I stopped in at High Desert Harley-Davidson® and chatted with a young lady named Emily, who helped me with selecting my poker chips. We talked about horses. She raises horses. We shared some horse stories, and she was a genuinely nice young lady to engage in conversation. I gave her one of my Ride for Kids® cards so that she would know what it was and check it out. She also said, hey, maybe you could get some sponsorship or something with the dealership. Emily pointed me toward Hayleigh who pointed me to Hannah who came out and handed me a form so I could fill out and send it in and see if they wanted to support me. I never could get that done in a timely manner, but I did get to make my photo op outside afterwards.

When I got back out on the highway, I noticed several tractor-trailer rigs were hauling hay that was in the big rolls for transport somewhere else. It seems that a lot of those trucks were on the road in this particular area of Idaho. There are a lot of scenic views that you just cannot get from inside "cages", but it's just a vast expanse getting out in country like this when you're on a motorcycle as opposed to in a "cage" (a car). I did take a picture of one of the cattle guards there on US 20 in Idaho.

Some of you may not know what a cattle guard is but it is interesting that it is where a fence comes to the road on each side and then there is the cattle guard, so traffic does not stop, but cows are fearful of crossing it. Cattle guards are used for the containment of livestock on the range as well as across driveways into farms back East.

If you have never been around a farm with livestock, this cattle guard device may be unfamiliar and you may ask, "What good does it do?". Cattle and horses and some other hoofed animals do not see things the same as humans and cannot assess what they see with the depth perception we have, so this becomes a visual barrier and something the animal does not want to traverse and get stuck. It has worked well to use them instead of gates when fence lines cross roadways or drives, with only the occasional wanderer jumping the guard.

Apparently, I did not realize I was at the elevation as high as it was when I crossed the area between Boise and Fairfield. There is another elevation that's kind of wide-open flat space and it is above a mile at 5527 feet, but it just does not look like that when you think about it. Then, it was into the Sawtooth National Forest and the incredibly beautiful country there. I was still looking at blue skies and white puffies when I reached Fairfield, Idaho when I stopped in at the Wrangler Drive-In, a great place for lunch. I had their fish and chips special which was very tasty, and it was a good lunch stop. It was kind of funny that I did leave my dash cam on and it kept taking pictures of the front of the drive-in and, of course, me and everybody else walking by. All the people walking in and out was interesting and I had to laugh because they are just a bunch of pictures that I have to just archive and not worry about until later.

After I left the Wrangler Drive-In, I got behind another box again, so that's just kind of the way it went from there. Riding through Carey was not only interesting, but rather speedy. There was a fancy Entering Carey sign and what seemed like just down the street, there was an equally fancy Leaving Carey sign. [90]

After leaving Carey, just around a bend in the road, I found myself riding into a valley that was just kind of crazy because what I kept seeing were these dark chocolate and black types of rock formations. Rubble is what it looked like stretched out across this valley to the South of US 20 and all the sagebrush growing on it almost like huge trucks just dumped large amounts of this rubble in the valley and the sagebrush grew over it all. It turns out I remembered that this must be Craters of the Moon and then I got to the sign that said it was Craters of the Moon National Monument and Preserve.

It is just a lot of volcanic rock formations there and you could see that it was not like I thought it was at first and it went on for miles and miles. I went through the park and took the loop ride and had the dash cam on to take a bunch of pictures of various things inside the park and it was it was pretty awesome. I certainly enjoyed it. [91]

At Craters of the Moon, in the gift shop, Sarah Lilly was the young lady who helped me with post cards and a patch. She was planning on getting married and she liked my wedding ring. I told her about it and that it was from Groove Life and was woodgrain silicone. She said it was the second one she had seen that day and I replied that it was the only alternative for me. I was then going to go take a quick ride through Craters of the Moon on their loop ride.

Then after leaving the Craters of the Moon, I went over to the little town of Arco, Idaho which, me being an electrical engineer working in the nuclear industry for the last thirty-eight years, it definitely piqued my interest. The interest in Arco was because it was the world's first nuclear powered city. [92]

I was also trying to get to the Experimental Breeder Reactor number one (EBR-1), which is where they first generated electrical energy from a nuclear power source. The fact that Arco and I were "born" in the same year, I had to go see what I could see. Even though the road was closed for EBR 1, I had to go as close as I could. [93] [94]

The Idaho National Laboratory (INL) entrance was across US 20 from EBR-1 and I passed by heading East toward Idaho Falls. I had been to the INL offices in Idaho Falls years ago when I went out there to assist the engineering group with specifications development, but I had not made it out to the actual geographical site. [95] [96]

With about 60 miles to go to reach Idaho Falls, I went past East Butte and Middle Butte and the eastern edge of the Idaho National Laboratory property and then came into Idaho Falls. [97] In Idaho Falls I found the Grand Teton Harley-Davidson® dealership and made my photo op there and picked out my poker chips. My goal was to get to Ashton, Idaho, and the Eagle Peak Lodge for the night, which is North of Idaho Falls towards West Yellowstone, Montana. That was one of my destination stops for the next day, so Eagle Peak Lodge it was. It was laundry day, so I found out that there was a laundromat right next to the restaurant that I had wanted to go to, so I went down there, took my laundry and was doing laundry while I ate dinner. It was a really great dinner and the laundry got done in time and I went back to the hotel and sorted things out so I could have a good night's sleep and that was the end of Day 16.

Heading
Toward
Boise

High
Desert
Harley-
Davidson®

Cattle guards for containment on the range

Does this look like a 5527 foot elevation?

Wrangler
Drive In,
a great
place for
lunch

Carey,
Idaho

Rounding
the bend
into Craters
of the Moon

Craters of
the Moon
National
Monument
and
Preserve

Craters
of the
Moon
Loop
Ride

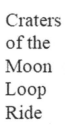

Craters
of the
Moon
Loop
Ride

The
road
was
closed
for
EBR 1

Idaho
National
Laboratory
Entrance

Entering
Arco,
Idaho

Entering
Idaho
Falls,
Idaho

Grand Teton Harley-Davidson®

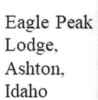

Eagle Peak Lodge, Ashton, Idaho

Day 17

Plan

Day	Starting Point / Ending Point	Miles / Ride Time	Potential Lodging	Potential Dining at Destination	Potential Attractions En Route
17 (Sat, July 25)	Ashton, ID Thermopolis, WY	285 6:24	Days Inn; Best Western; Two Rivers Inn; Roundtop Mountain Motel; Quality Inn	One-Eyed Buffalo Brewing Co Inc; Thermopolis Café; Black Bear Café; The Front Porch	• Early breakfast (0600) at Trails Inn Restaurant for time in Yellowstone (Take-out); • Gas up in West Yellowstone, MT; • Yellowstone National Park; • Lunch in the Park at Old Faithful General Store Grill or Old Faithful Snow Lodge Geyser Grill (Take-out) Visit with Don Small; • Buffalo Bill Center of the West, Cody, WY; • Buffalo Bill H-D, Cody, WY; • Gas up in Cody; • Wyoming Dinosaur Center, Thermopolis, WY (if before 1700) • Mass online somewhere

Actual

Day	Starting Point / Ending Point	Miles / Ride Time	Lodging	Dining at Destination	Attractions En Route
17 (Sat, July 25)	Ashton, ID Worland, WY	235 5:24	Days Inn	Blair's Supermarket	• Gas up in Ashton, ID; • Breakfast with JoAnn Lawson and husband Paul at Running Bear Pancake House, West Yellowstone, MT; • Gas up in West Yellowstone, MT; • Yellowstone National Park; • Old Faithful Eruption; • Lunch in the Park at Grant Village Campground General Store (Take-out) Visit with Don Small; • Gas up in Greybull, WY; • Mass online somewhere • Supper from Blairs Super Market at motel (Take-out)

Leaving out of Eagle Peak Lodge heading up in this section US 20 heads North towards West Yellowstone, Montana where you typically get into Yellowstone National Park. US 20, which takes you into Wyoming to the right, or to the East of West Yellowstone, also runs through the park toward Cody, Wyoming. So, for a while, I was headed North to West Yellowstone and through the Targhee National Forest with lots of wonderful tall trees and some wide-open spaces. I use that term "wide-open spaces" a lot, don't I? After that heading towards Montana and the mountains in the distance was such a beautiful sight to see.

The goal for the morning was to meet some friends (that I had worked with at the Savannah River Site years back) for breakfast in West Yellowstone. My friend, JoAnn, and her husband Paul were vacationing in Idaho and we had been communicating during my trip and said, "OK, let's meet at West Yellowstone and have breakfast". I met them there at the Running Bear Pancake House which was an excellent breakfast stop and we visited for a while. It was good to see and visit some friends in West Yellowstone along the way on this 10,000 plus mile trip. West Yellowstone again is how you get into Yellowstone Park from the West side of the park. The lines were not too bad, but having a National Parks Senior Pass, I could get into a lane and slide into Yellowstone rather quickly. Inside the park, US 20 is only marked maybe in just a few places because technically, it is not in the park, but the road actually does go through there. So, they have a few markers, but generally you must know where you going to stay on the US highway route.

The Madison River runs in the park which presents a very serene somewhat soothing effect as the road winds along the river. Some very scenic views presented themselves along the Madison River and I thoroughly enjoyed seeing them all.

> "The Gibbon and Firehole rivers join to form the Madison River. The Madison flows to Hebgen Lake, joins the Jefferson River and eventually the Missouri River on its way to the Gulf of Mexico." [98]

Riding farther along, I came across, more than once, where cars were slowed down and jammed up traffic and it made me wonder what was up ahead and, usually, it was probably some wildlife that folks were slowing down to take a look and see. Also, in Yellowstone there are mountains as well as the valleys, rivers, lakes, and streams which are all wonderful to view as well.

It was good to see bikers in Yellowstone and I met up with a few of those headed the opposite direction. As I rode through the park, I also noticed the ever-changing landscape. Depending on where you go, there were some wide-open spaces in plains and the mountains in the distance and it is really quite remarkable. There was road work even in Yellowstone and I could not seem to get away from it anywhere. Heading towards Old Faithful, I was hoping to catch one of the gushes that it routinely is noted to perform. The plan for afterwards was going to go see a friend of mine, who is from Augusta, who works in Yellowstone every summer, and touch base with him for lunch. Reaching the Old Faithful site, the schedule indicated that it was going to be spouting off about 12:18 or something like that and it was a little after 12:00 when I saw the sign, so I decided to stick around and watch. Just like clockwork, I got to see Old Faithful spout off and then not too far from there was the Grant Park Campground where my friend was working. We met up at the Campground General Store and ate lunch at the tables outside since we bought prepackaged sandwiches from the store. I enjoyed sitting there and visiting my friend, Don Small, and we had a pleasant time to visit. Then it was time to get on the move again, so we bid farewell and parted the campground.

As I said before, there were more changes in scenery than you could imagine and the sky had some white puffies come in and some were threatening to get thick, but I still had blue sky behind them. Even in the darkness where it covered the sun, you could see where it was blue sky up ahead. The weather seemed to change as much as the scenery.

Another attraction in Yellowstone was my unplanned detour to Canyon Village area, which provided another view and photo opportunity. What do I mean by "unplanned" you ask? Remember I mentioned that US 20 is not marked but in a few locations? Well, my unplanned detour to Canyon village area was basically a result of not realizing I was passing the turn to maintain the course on US 20 and riding on straight ahead. When I saw the sign for Canyon Village, I knew I had gone a bridge too far, so to speak. At least that detour provided an opportunity to have more views and more pictures and more experience of Yellowstone. It also required me to back track and come back around to catch up to the turn off that took me to Fishing Bridge. Upon reaching Fishing Bridge, of course, there was major construction there which had a section of dirt and gravel and potholes. The sign said "Bump", but that was really an understatement, especially on a motorcycle, but anyway I survived it and got through.

Riding along Yellowstone Lake also provided the opportunity to see yet another body of water in Yellowstone and the accompanying beauty of the scenery. [99]

Shortly after that, I met up with a bison on the side of the road grazing and you know folks would stop to take a look and to get photographs. Of course, the photo that I have does not really show how close he was to me, on a motorcycle. You have all probably seen the words on car and truck mirrors that states, "Objects are closer than they appear", right? Well, that is the case here with my dash cam. The way my camera takes pictures, basically it could have a sign at the bottom of every photo that says objects are closer than they appear because it does not look like he is really close. When you think about it, I was in one lane of a two-lane road and he was only across on the edge of the opposite lane, so only one lane was in between us. Since he was right on the edge of the road, as I was going by, he was awfully close and noticeably big, so I kept going. The photo caption, "Approaching the Grazing Buffalo" stems from the commonplace association of the animal with the western songs and folklore, but I have actually seen it on road signs. [100]

For a long stretch of road after that the weather was changing again with thick clouds and blue skies poking through and peeking out from behind clouds quite often. The clouds were just there, but I did not get rained on. Riding by Mary Bay was another scenic experience and later, there was a whole lot of traffic in one little area where folks were standing around and, I guess, they were hoping to see elk or buffalo (bison) or something. I managed to get through that, and I rode into an area that was a lake in the mountains with twisties. What a great combination.

The clouds were continuing to thicken a little, but I could still see blue sky behind, so I kept heading towards Cody, Wyoming and the clouds started getting thicker and as I crossed Sylvan Pass, which is the highest point of US 20 at 8524 feet [101]. Of course, being as high as it is in the mountains affects how the clouds dump rain, so those seemingly innocent clouds started to rain a little bit and water drops danced on the windshield as I exited Yellowstone. It really was not a very hard rain, but just enough to be a nuisance.

Seeing the light crossing the Shoshone River, I rolled into the Shoshone National Forest and went through the Wapiti Palisades area still heading out towards Cody, Wyoming. That means I was passing the Wapiti Palisades area along the North Fork of the Shoshone River while outrunning the storm toward Cody. I could see the light through the clouds and the blue sky behind it was encouraging as I went through the Wapiti Valley along the Buffalo Bill Reservoir. There were several tunnels there and a pretty interesting tunnel picture showing red as I traveled through it. I am not sure why the lighting does what it does for the camera, but it was a pretty interesting light show.

Cody came into view not too long after the dam and reservoir and I could still see clouds to the North heading crossways behind me catching up to me somewhat. Cody is the "Rodeo Capitol of the World, by the way. [102] I had to make an obligatory Walmart stop for miscellaneous supplies, and after I came out of Walmart, the edge of the rain was starting to catch up. That being said, I hightailed it out of Cody and bypassed going to Buffalo Bill Harley-Davidson® just to get out of town and not to have to deal with the weather.

After Cody, I was going along fairly well until US 20 headed South, which meant that the wind and rain caught up to me going crossways this time. It was not so much rain as it was the wind which was just really howling. The sun was going down and as the sun was going down behind me, everything started to have a red glow in front of me, which was the effect of the red setting sun reflecting off the wispy rain that was in the air. It did not really rain hard, but it was just kind of a mist that glowed red as I went through there. As I turned South, it became crossways as I was trying to head towards Thermopolis, Wyoming. I did not make it to Thermopolis; however, because I saw that there was a Days Inn in Worland and that is where I stayed for the night, instead of going 33 more miles to Thermopolis. Something to eat was next on the agenda as it was already after 9 o'clock at night. Nothing much was open for dinner, actually, nothing much was open at all, but I found Blair's Grocery and I was able to get something to eat to take back to the room.

After that, as per usual, I performed the nightly deeds with the photo transfer and such.

Heading up
to West
Yellowstone

Heading
to
Montana

Heading
East to
my
Breakfast
Location

West
Yellowstone
Montana

The
Advantage
of Having
a Senior
Pass

Scene
along
the
Madison
River

More
Scenes
along
the
Madison
River

Oh how
the
scenery
changes

Awaiting On Old Faithful Which Did Not Disappoint

Riding
along
Yellowstone
Lake

Unplanned
Detour to
Canyon
Village

Approaching
the Grazing
Buffalo

Mary
Bay

Near
Sylvan
Pass

Passing
the
Wapiti
Palisades

Seeing the light crossing the Shoshone River

Wapiti Valley along the Buffalo Bill Reservoir

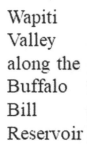

Tunnel
next to
the
Buffalo
Bill
Dam

Interesting
lighting
effect in
the tunnel

Cody is the "Rodeo Capitol of the World."

Obligatory visit to Walmart before the storm catches up to me

Day 18

Plan

Day	Starting Point / Ending Point	Miles / Ride Time	Potential Lodging	Potential Dining at Destination	Potential Attractions En Route
18 (Sun, July 26)	Thermopolis, WY Box Elder, SD	450 7:42	Jordon and Mallory's Light of Mine Ranch		• Breakfast at Thermopolis Café (Take-out); • Mills, WY; • Oil City H-D, Casper, WY (Permanently Closed / possible photo op) • Lunch at Sherrie's Place, Casper, WY (Take-out); • Gas up in Casper; • Jackalope Square, Douglas, WY; • Stagecoach Museum, Lusk, WY; • Gas stop at Sinclair, 301 S Main, Lusk, WY; • Crazy Horse Memorial at Fort Robinson, Harrison, NE; • Run up to Mount Rushmore Memorial, Keystone, SD; • Visit Jordan and Mallory at Light of Mine Ranch, Box Elder, SD (Overnight)

Actual

Day	Starting Point / Ending Point	Miles / Ride Time	Lodging	Dining at Destination	Attractions En Route
18 (Sun, July 26)	Worland, WY Box Elder, SD	450 7:42	Jordon and Mallory's Light of Mine Ranch		• Breakfast at Days Inn, Worland, WY; • Mills, WY; • Gas up in Mills, WY; • Breakfast/Brunch at G'Ma's Diner, Mills, WY (Dine-In); • Jackalope Square, Douglas, WY; • Gas stop at Sinclair, 301 S Main, Lusk, WY; • Crazy Horse Memorial at Fort Robinson, Harrison, NE (Viewed from bike); • Ride up to Mount Rushmore Memorial, Keystone, SD; • Visit Jordan and Mallory at Light of Mine Ranch, Box Elder, SD (Overnight)

Last night I had to cut it short and stopped in Worland, Wyoming instead of going 33 more miles to Thermopolis. The wind was just starting to really blow me around and it was starting to get dark, so I said, "Days Inn, there you go, I'm in." Then I went to Blair's Grocery to get some something to eat because everything else was closed up for the night. It was getting close to 10 o'clock and they would close at 10:00, but I made it and picked up dinner for the motel room.

Stopping short of Thermopolis also meant that plans for Mass had to change. I had not checked prior to the trip for Masses in Worland since I had not planned on stopping there. After the fact, I learned that there were several Catholic churches in Worland, but the timing was totally off to make it to any of them. Without much of an internet connection and the fact that it became extremely late very fast, I ended up using the travel dispensation. That, coupled with needing to make it to my nephew's house early enough on Sunday to have a meaningful visit, prompted my decision.

After the stormy weather the night before, the shining sun was a great start for the day with wide open skies as I crossed the Bighorn River. I left Worland early without really having any breakfast food around, so I had a granola bar and did not worry about it.

Thermopolis is home of the world's largest mineral hot springs, the Wyoming Dinosaur Center, the northern end of the Wind River Canyon and many other western attractions. Thermopolis is also dinosaur country and, at least for this traveler, road construction, since there was a good bit of it in town. Thermopolis is the northern entrance to the Wind River Canyon, which is a two-lane road with steep walls and river a long way below, so winters could get pretty scary. It was especially scary seeing a sign which read, "(US) 20 Closed, Return to Thermopolis when flashing". [103]

Riding through the Wind River Canyon reminded me of riding along the Arkansas River where the whole time I was traveling South on US 20 I thought I was going downhill, but when I got to the end of the Canyon there was a dam in front of me. I was looking at the low side of the dam with the water behind it which says the river is coming at me and I said, "there's no way", but it does. The Wind River flows North and just the way that the rock formations are and the way the road is so high compared to the River you really could not see which way the water was flowing. Unlike on the Arkansas River where I knew that the river was flowing towards me and I knew that I was headed uphill, but the optical illusion said I was going downhill. In the Wind River Canyon there are markers along the way for the different historical periods of the sediment layers and so forth, so you can tell where you are in the history of the formations. I did leave the dash cam on the whole time and my plan was to string all those pictures together into some kind of high-speed ride through the canyon video, but someday maybe. [104]

Just before getting into the Boysen Reservoir area, again I was taken aback when I saw the dam for the first time, but then I saw the reservoir area, which is wide-open and very stunning. The country around there as US 20 turns back towards the East is wide open (there is that term again) flat land for a long way near Shoshoni. Then, after riding through the town I came upon another one of those signs that I saw at Thermopolis heading into the Wind River Canyon, but this one was just out into the plains, but it says "(US) 20 is closed when this is flashing turn back and go to Shoshoni" so it must be for snow accumulation in that area.

Since breakfast was almost non-existent, after stopping for gas, I found myself in a little town called Mills, Wyoming, fancy that! I happened to see a restaurant called G-Ma's Diner and it seemed like it would be a good place to have a later breakfast. Looking across the street, I saw the nearest police station, so I realized then that I was in Mills, Wyoming. Cool. I had an exceptionally good breakfast, by the way,

After that good breakfast, I motored off to Douglas, Wyoming to see Jackalope Square. In Jackalope Square they have a large replica of a jackalope – supposedly, a cross between a jack rabbit and an antelope. There is some history behind this jackalope in the area around Douglas and it is kind of funny, so that is what they claim anyway. [105]

Riding around town to see the sights, I stopped at a convenience store and picked up some postcards from Wyoming that showed the Wapiti Palisades, which is the area heading into Yellowstone from Cody. I saw the Wapiti Palisades as I was going out of Yellowstone. So, I started trying to find a place to write those up and get them mailed sometime soon. It seemed it was impossible to get away from the construction and there was one of those portable traffic lights that they set up when there is construction going on. It was one of those "Single Lanes Ahead" and so forth, but oh well, that is the way it goes. At this time heading back out on the highway I kind of got a yearning for some of the twisties, because I had a lot of long straight roads for quite a way.

Riding parallel to the railroad lines on US 20 is kind of funny because the tracks are supposed to be owned by one railroad company, but the engines that I saw were from another railroad company. I learned later that it is just like this fascinating board game we used to play in college called "Rail Baron", which says, basically, you charge other railroad companies to travel on your tracks. The section of track shown in the photo that follows was supposedly owned by Burlington Northern San Francisco (BNSF), but the engines sported a Union Pacific (UP) logo on them, so I am sure that they had to pay a price to transport on that track. Fully loaded coal trains were heading back East like me, and I would see empty cars coming back to the West, so they were coal mining out there and taking the coal back East. I had trains around there. I had highway. I was on my bike. I had bikers that were in the vicinity and blue skies. What more could you ask for?

One of the photos that follows shows another full load heading East with a pusher engine to help the two up front. Union Pacific locomotives are running on BNSF tracks at this point, so a little history of each is in the back of the book. I did a little research and found that, while actual tracks are owned and maintained by one railroad company, the other company can pay to run on the rails of that company. They each gouge the other, but come together to lobby in Washington, D.C. [106] [107] [108]

Lusk, Wyoming was the next spot on the travel map, which again, was wide-open flatland, but it was 5000 feet in elevation, so it is really interesting and still somewhat mind-boggling. Then, after finding a post office to mail some post cards, I went to the center of town and filled up before heading out again. US 20 makes a right turn there and a few blocks down I saw that "Historic Wyoming US 20" sign, which was cool, but then when I got there, they had taken up all the pavement from both lanes. It was dirt, gravel, and potholes for 9 1/2 miles! That was an interesting 9 1/2 miles with the speed limit at 45 at first and I said, "No way I'm going over 35!" Even at that I was still having to deal with the squirrelly mess of the gravel and dirt and the potholes that kind of bounce you around on a motorcycle. I did not care that the speed limit was 45 mph, I was not going over 35 on that road surface, so those behind just had to be patient on the one-lane road. That was not so much fun, but nine and a half miles was a still pretty awesome ride experience, so I said, "let's see what happens next."

The town of Lusk was founded in 1886 by Frank S. Lusk (1857-1930). [109]

Anyway, I made it to the Nebraska state line after reaching some pavement again and riding along in wide open plains and I saw this one tree that was on the side of the road – "The Lone Tree on the Prairie" right on the South side of the road. It was interesting to see the one tree right there all by itself.

After riding through Chadron, Nebraska, I rolled into Robinson, Nebraska and saw the pyramid style stone structure out in the field there that is a monument to Crazy Horse who died there at Fort Robinson. It was kind of tragic the way that ended up even after all the issue with the Battle of Little Bighorn and Custer and so forth. Almost shameful how Crazy Horse had to die the way he did there at Fort Robinson. In one of the photos that follow, the cabin location of the tragic death of Crazy Horse at Fort Robinson is shown. [110]

Prior to leaving home on this journey, I had made arrangements with my nephew, who lives with his wife and family outside of Rapid City, South Dakota, that I would come visit and spend the night, so I headed up to South Dakota. From Chadron, I went into South Dakota and my nephew had told me, "If you're going to come here and see us, you have to go to Mount Rushmore on the way." So that was where I headed first and I still had sunshine, blue skies and white puffies just about all the way into the town of Hot Springs, South Dakota. Hot Springs is a fascinating little town. Somewhere along the way, I saw a sign warning that "Buffalo are dangerous" and I said to myself, "You really gotta remind people of that?" [Notice that the state calls them buffalo]. [111]

Oh well, then I captured another picture with a better view of a cattle guard right on top of it so that folks can understand what a cattle guard really does. It really is kind of a visual barrier to cattle and horses for the most part as well but mostly it is for the cattle because they do not want to get stuck in the in the rails.

Custer, South Dakota is another interesting little town I passed through after riding by the Crazy Horse Mountain Memorial and saw the start of the carving for that monument. It was off in the distance and I did not really have a chance to go in because I was limited on time and wanted to get to my nephew's before it got too late in the evening and also before dark. [112] [113]

Finally, I made it to the entrance to Mount Rushmore [114] and went in to take a couple of photos and I picked up some postcards, so that I could send them back to the grandkids. I also picked up a couple patches for the motorcycle vest and then headed back out to Rapid City. My nephew's house is in Box Elder, outside of Rapid City to the East, and I made it in time for a great spaghetti and meatballs dinner (my nephew's wife really makes an exceptionally good spaghetti sauce). We had a good visit and, of course, they wanted to see what the map looked like where I was tracing all my travels. I opened the map up on the dinner table and it was really fun to go through it and I had to mark up where I had been that day, so that it was up to date.

My nephew and his wife do a lot with foster care there in Box Elder, working on building a charity program, non-profit organization for the "Light of Mine Ranch" [115] to promote better conditions and better ways to deal with foster care and foster parenting. He has got a mission ahead of him for that, so I really hold that in high regard.

Entering
Thermopolis,
Wyoming

First
time
seeing
a sign
like
this

Wind
River
Canyon
was
awesome

Believe
it or not
the
river is
flowing
toward
me

Tunnel
fun in
the
canyon

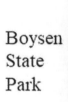
Boysen
State
Park

Wide
open
Wyoming

Another
one of
those
scary
signs

Mills, Wyoming has a police force and a
great breakfast restaurant, G-Ma's Diner.

Jackalope
Square

Missing the twisties a little bit at this point

Railroads played a major part in Westward expansion

Entering
Lusk,
Wyoming
at over
5000 feet
elevation

Historic
Wyoming
US 20
sign, but
little did I
know
what laid
in wait
ahead

Over nine
miles of no
pavement is
what laid in
wait for me

Nebraska
State
Line

The
lone
tree on
the
prairie

Crazy
Horse
memorial
in the
distance

South
Dakota
State
Line

Fall
River in
Hot
Springs,
South
Dakota

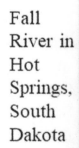

A closer
look at
cattle
guards
mentioned
previously

Making
the turn
in
Custer,
South
Dakota

Mount Rushmore Memorial

Day 19

Plan

Day	Starting Point / Ending Point	Miles / Ride Time	Potential Lodging	Potential Dining at Destination	Potential Attractions En Route
19 (Mon, July 27)	Box Elder, SD	497	Holiday Inn Sioux City;	Jim's Burgers;	• Second breakfast at Helen's Pancake & Steak House (Take-out)
	Sioux City, IA	8:16	Ramada Inn Sioux City;	The Diving Elk;	• (Laundry Day – Spin-N-Go Laundromat)
			Super 8;	Perkins Restaurant;	• Gas stop at Road Runner Shell Travel Center, Valentine, NE;
			Sioux City Hotel;	IHOP	• Sellors Barton Museum, Ainsworth, NE;
			Courtyard by Marriott;		• Lunch at D & B Cafe, Ainsworth, NE (Take-out);
					• Gas stop at Casey's in O'Neill, NE;
	Alternative O'Neill, NE	366	Holiday Inn Express;		• (Alternative Overnight Stop in O'Neill, NE)
		5:55	Super 8		

Actual

Day	Starting Point / Ending Point	Miles / Ride Time	Lodging	Dining at Destination	Attractions En Route
19 (Mon, July 27)	Box Elder, SD	366	Holiday Inn Express	Westside Restaurant	• Black Hills H-D, Rapid City, SD;
	O'Neill, NE	5:55			• Sturgis H-D, Sturgis, SD;
					• Gas up in Sturgis, SD;
					• Gas up at Maverick in Chadron, NE;
					• Lunch at Maverick in Chadron, NE?;
					• Gas stop at Sandhill Oil Company -Dino Mart, Valentine, NE;
					• Supper at Westside Restaurant (Nebraska Steak) (Dine-In)

After having a good breakfast and having some time with the kids and the obligatory "Let's take a picture on the motorcycle" type of experience, (everybody had to have a chance to get their picture on the motorcycle) I headed out towards Rapid City. It was a beautiful, blue sky day and not hardly any clouds anywhere as I rode down Main Street in Rapid City. They have life size bronze statues of the Presidents of the United States, and maybe have some others as well, but supposedly they are there on various street corners. I went through and saw some of the statues and, of course, there was construction in downtown Rapid City. I did a post office run to drop off the postcards to send back to the grandkids and one more time I left the dash cam on and caught myself coming out of the post office (That picture will not be included here).

Being as close as I was, I had to make the trip to the Black Hills Harley-Davidson® dealership in Rapid City and I got my shirt, poker chips and photo op there and observed they were getting ready for the Sturgis rally the week before it was supposed to start. They were getting prepared with all the parking tents, vendor booths and so forth right outside of the building. Then again, since I was so close, about 20 miles or so to the North, was Sturgis, so yeah, I had to take that journey. I was so close I had to do it, so I went up to Sturgis Harley-Davidson® and did the same thing there. I got my got my T-shirt, poker chips and photo op and then headed out of Sturgis back down to Chadron, Nebraska.

Now that I was heading East again, a gas and lunch stop was in order, so that became the activity in Chadron. Near there were more of the Nebraska plains just like some of them in other states. Along the way were railroad tracks running beside US 20 and there are some railroad tracks that are still in service and some that are not. A stop in Valentine, Nebraska allowed for refueling and relieving, so it was a good thing. [116]

The sandhills were alive with corn, so you realize all this talk about cornhuskers being Nebraskans was definitely evident, but there were other crops growing in the area as well.

Of course, I got behind another box and as in some other times on the eastward journey, in the afternoon, your shadows get long in front of you. I reached O'Neill, Nebraska and stayed there and had dinner at the Westside Restaurant. I had to have a Nebraska steak because I was in Nebraska beef country, so that was what I did. O'Neill is supposedly the "Irish Capital of Nebraska", so in the center of town they have painted on the intersection (it kind of covers the whole intersection) a big old shamrock. It appears in one of the photos that follow and it is painted over the entire intersection (the stem is just above my shadow with the lobes to the left). [117]

After dinner I went back to the hotel and did my thing with the pictures and so forth and had a good night's sleep.

Box Elder to Rapid City, South Dakota

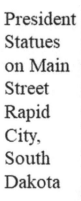

President Statues on Main Street Rapid City, South Dakota

Black
Hills
Harley-
Davidson®
preparing
for Sturgis
Bike
Week

Black
Hills
Harley-
Davidson®
photo op

Sturgis
Harley-
Davidson®

Sturgis
Harley-
Davidson®
photo op

Back to
Nebraska

Chadron
for the
second
time

Some
rails are
still in
use and
some
are not

Valentine,
Nebraska

Entering
O'Neill,
the Irish
Capital of
Nebraska

Shamrock
painted
over the
entire
intersection

Plan

Day	Starting Point / Ending Point	Miles / Ride Time	Potential Lodging	Potential Dining at Destination	Potential Attractions En Route
20a (Tue, July 28)	Sioux City, IA Ames, IA Alternative O'Neill, NE	188 3:13 319 5:36	N/A	Lunch at Hickory Park, Ames, IA	• Alternative breakfast at Westside Restaurant, O'Neill, NE (Take-out); • Breakfast at Scooter's Coffee, Sioux City, IA (Take-out); • Rooster's H-D, Sioux City, IA; • World's Largest Popcorn Ball, Sac City, IA; • Gas stop at Phillips 66 near Webster City; • Lunch at Hickory Park, Ames, IA (Dine-In); • Zylstra H-D, Ames, IA (Opens at 12:00)
20b (Tue, July 28)	Ames, IA (East) Dubuque, IL	181 2:47	Quality Inn East Dubuque; Days Inn by Wyndham Dubuque; Holiday Inn Dubuque/ Galena;	Caroline's Restaurant; Sunshine Family Restaurant	• Silver Eagle H-D, Waterloo, IA; • Gas up at Love's Travel Stop in Waterloo; • National Farm Toy Museum, Dyersville, IA; • Field of Dreams Movie Site, Dyersville, IA; • McGrath Dubuque H-D, Dubuque, IA (If before 1800); • (Slip into Wisconsin from East Dubuque, IL after check-in)

Actual

Day	Starting Point / Ending Point	Miles / Ride Time	Lodging	Dining at Destination	Attractions En Route
20 (Tue, July 28)	O'Neill, NE Dubuque, IA	476 7:40	Hampton Inn, Dubuque, IA	Sunshine Family Restaurant	• Gas up at Casey's in O'Neill, NE; • Rooster's H-D, Sioux City, IA; • World's Largest Popcorn Ball, Sac City, IA; • Gas stop at Casey's Sac City, IA; • Lunch at Tom Thumb Drive-In, Fort Dodge, IA (Dine-In); • Silver Eagle H-D, Waterloo, IA; • Gas up at Casey's in Waterloo; • National Farm Toy Museum, Dyersville, IA (After Hours);

Day	Starting Point / Ending Point	Miles / Ride Time	Lodging	Dining at Destination	Attractions En Route
					• Field of Dreams Movie Site, Dyersville, IA (Rode through); • Supper from HyVee convenience store

Of course, as before, heading East in the morning I once again found myself riding into the sun, this time out of O'Neill, Nebraska. Riding by the farms and the farm mechanization and all of that is very noteworthy to me. My recently deceased uncle in Virginia had a farm that he cobbled together from scratch from a house that started out with a dirt floor and kept on building up and doing things differently, based on what was most profitable. He changed from having an egg route for the Virginia Dairy around Richmond, Virginia and had several chicken houses where we would go help collect the eggs. This was back before it was mechanized, where you had to pull the hens off the roost and get the eggs and take them in baskets to the only machine that my uncle had at that time. It was the mechanized grader where we would wash them and look at them and they would be graded for large, extra-large, and so forth. We would then box them up and he would take him to the Virginia Dairy for distribution. Those were fun times for kids growing up combining work with playing with my cousins.

He changed from that minimal automation and began building up with mechanized feeders for the chickens and a lot of the process became mechanized simply because he did not have enough hands to get all the work done in a timely fashion. He then migrated from that to raising beef cattle and hogs and grew his own silage and had several of the big blue Harvestore® silos that stored the silage until it was needed to feed the cattle in the feed lot. The setup included a mechanized conveyor feeder which, by screw conveyor trough, dropped silage out at designated spots where the cattle would come up to feed. I remember he had some huge tractors, some no till planters, and a lot of things were mechanized over the years, but it was fun to go to visit and go help out where we could. I think I drove one of the tractors at nine-years-old when we were building a barbed wire fence. Fun times indeed.

My memory was jogged as I was riding through Nebraska with all the different mechanization techniques that they have nowadays to help farmers actually produce their crops, so I had to share the story about my uncle. I saw lots of mechanized irrigation techniques that were just awesome to see the massiveness of the water distribution that was available there. Soon I was able to see the second "Lone Tree on the Prairie", off to the South, not necessarily as close as the last one, but it was funny that it almost looked the same, but it was definitely a different tree. For miles, I could see the highway and the sun up ahead and blue skies and white puffies floating around and it was really a beautiful day. I saw some more farm mechanization along the way on this route and, of course, construction and a box up ahead, but then it was not long before I rolled into Iowa at Sioux City.

A stop at Rooster's Harley-Davidson® in Sioux City, Iowa became part of the modified plan because it was later in the day on Tuesday, and they were open. I had not planned on being able to stop there because they were not going to be open the day and time that I would come through based on the original plan of making it to Sioux City Monday night. As things shifted around, I did not get as far as Sioux City and since O'Neill was a planned alternative stopping point, I stayed there Monday night. Staying in Sioux City on

Monday night would have meant that I would have to leave before Rooster's opened up on Tuesday morning, but this way I got to Rooster's when they were open. Another set of poker chips and a shirt became the rewards for being a day late.

One thing I did use a lot was Google Maps in the planning for this trip, but occasionally, it left me hanging. Heading into Sioux City to get to Rooster's was one of those times where it says, "turn here" and I turn there, and it goes up over little hill and then it looks like it is just a dirt and gravel road for a long way to get to the end point. I said no I am not going to do that this time because I have a choice, so I chose a more paved, but longer route to get to Rooster's.

While choosing my poker chips at Rooster's, I talked with Tanya, who has on her name tag "T", so we were talking about "T David" and I gave her a Ride for Kids® card. We chatted for a bit, and then I paid the restroom an obligatory visit, secured my photo op out front and then headed out on the highway once again.

The Iowa landscape east of Sioux City was again a lot of farmland as I took to the open road once again. US 20 has been modernized in Iowa quite a bit and they have taken the route off of the old road and made it an almost superhighway on the route it takes now. I wanted to go into Sac City to see the Old Town and also to go by the World's Largest Popcorn Ball, which was awesome, so I found the old route. The old Route 20 goes through Sac City, but the new highway kind of bypasses it, so you must go off the road about three miles to get to the actual town. I found the world's largest popcorn ball across from Casey's where I got gas, so it was pretty cool. By that time, it was noon, but I was not really ready to eat lunch, so I thought I would just have a little snack or something after filling up the tank with gas.

Not too long after that, I stopped and had a great lunch in Fort Dodge at Tom Thumb Burgers and met up with an old biker who was heading to Sturgis again as he had done for over thirty years in a row. He said folks in his nearby small town refer to him as "Mister Sturgis" because his entire wardrobe from head to toe is "Sturgis" apparel. We had a great conversation about traveling on two wheels and his many years of riding and going to the annual rally in the Black Hills of South Dakota. Alvin is his name, and I do not know his last name, but they do call him "Mr. Sturgis". He still rides, but a kind of three wheeled step through machine now, but he talked a lot about all kinds of stuff, and he is planning to go to the rally again this year. He is a really interesting character and rides with the local Christian Motorcycle Association. We talked a good bit, and it was a pleasant experience. I hope I can figure out how to get back in touch with him. I gave him a Ride for Kids® card, so maybe he will figure out some way to contact me.

When I got into Waterloo, Iowa I stopped at the Silver Eagle Harley-Davidson® picked out my poker chips and set up my photo op there with blue skies and white puffies. After that, it was great to ride into an area that basically captured the day, as I could see for miles and miles, kind of like the song goes from "The Who". As I approached Dyersville, Iowa I saw by the sign on the highway that there is a Basilica of Saint Francis Xavier there, which I had not known about beforehand.

Dyersville is also home to the National Farm Toy Museum, which I wished I could have been there in time before they closed, but unfortunately, I could not. Dyersville is probably most famous for being home of the site of the movie "Field of Dreams". I did get to go see that, but just to drive through, not stopping to get off the bike and wouldn't you know that the road to the Field of Dreams entrance was under construction and had an extensive repaving going on? They had single file traffic led through by an escort vehicle, so it took a while to get there, but I did get there. The Field of Dreams site had a gravel driveway and parking lot area, but the dash cam did get photos of the building and the field and then I headed back out to the construction zone once more. I wanted to get back into town to actually see the Basilica of Saint Francis Xavier which I did, and it was fascinating to see. [118]

As I was headed for Dubuque, Iowa for the evening, which is on the East side of Iowa and, of course, there is construction as I motored closer to Dubuque, but I was able to get in there for the night. Thankful for the good weather all the way to the Dubuque area, I located the Hampton Inn, on the West side of town. It was available and worked out well as I walked to the grocery store, they call Hy Vee, I think it is, and got some barbecue boneless chicken wings and a quesadilla that came together, packaged from the deli. I also picked out some special apple raisin nut type of slaw that was really good. I tried to balance out a meal and heated it up in the microwave, except for the slaw, and, of course, I had a big Coors Light beer. So, it was then time for signing off and trying to get some sleep and that was the end of Day 20.

Mechanized
Agriculture

The
long
highway
ahead

Into
Iowa
at
Sioux
City

Sign
interpretation
is unpaved
road ahead

Roosters
Harley-
Davidson®
Sioux City

Roosters
Harley-
Davidson®
photo op.

Old
Town
Sac
City,
Iowa

World's
Largest
Popcorn
Ball

Silver
Eagle
Harley-
Davidson®
Waterloo

Silver
Eagle
Harley-
Davidson®
photo op

Field of
Dreams
Entrance

Field of
Dreams
Field

Basilica
of St.
Francis
Xavier

Into
Dubuque
under
construction

Day 21

Plan

Day	Starting Point / Ending Point	Miles / Ride Time	Potential Lodging	Potential Dining at Destination	Potential Attractions En Route
21 (Wed, July 29)	East Dubuque, IL Perrysburg, OH	435 10:28	Quality Inn; Comfort Suites Perrysburgh; La Quinta; EconoLodge; Baymont Inn	Cracker Barrel Panera Bread Bob Evans Burger King	• Breakfast at Sunshine Family Restaurant (Take-out) • Kegel H-D, Rockford, IL; • Gas up in Rockford, IL; • Illinois Railway Museum, Union, IL; • Lunch at Little Joes, Countryside, IL (Take-out); • Illinois H-D, Countryside, IL; • The Harley-Davidson® Shop of Michigan City, Michigan City, IN; • Slip into Michigan via US 127 • Toledo H-D (if before 1800); • Signature H-D, Perrysburg, OH (if before 1800);

Actual

Day	Starting Point / Ending Point	Miles / Ride Time	Lodging	Dining at Destination	Attractions En Route
21 (Wed, July 29)	Dubuque, IA Norwalk, OH	435 10:28	Norwalk Inn		• Breakfast at Hampton Inn, Dubuque, IA (Take-out); • McGrath Dubuque H-D photo op before opening; • Detour into Wisconsin due to US 20 Bridge work and back to Illinois on Hwy 35; • Kegel H-D, Rockford, IL; • Gas up in Rockford, IL; • Lunch at Little Joe's Italian Beef & Sausage, Countryside, IL (Dine-out); • Illinois H-D, Countryside, IL (On the Historical Route 66 road); • The Harley-Davidson® Shop of Michigan City, Michigan City, IN; • Slip into Michigan via US 127 • Toledo H-D (Photo op only); • Gas up at Speedway in Perrysburg, OH; • Sandwich supper at Speedway, Perrysburg (Take-out); • Signature H-D, Perrysburg, OH (Photo op only);

Well, I started out Wednesday morning in Dubuque by getting a photo op at the McGrath Dubuque Harley-Davidson®, before they opened. Heading out to the East on US 20, again, there was a detour. I had originally planned on trying to get to Wisconsin by just going up a road heading north just to claim that I had been in Wisconsin on this trip, but it appears that the Iowa/Illinois Departments of Transportation took care of that for me by closing the US 20 bridge from Iowa into Illinois. The detour took me a different route across the Mississippi into Wisconsin but brought me back on the same road I was going to use back and forth before there was knowledge of a detour. Crossing the Mississippi River into Wisconsin did not make me immune to the habit of getting behind a box; however, even on the little two-lane road for the detour.

The detour took me back to real live US 20 in Illinois, so I got into Illinois and back on US 20 now rolling into Galena, Illinois, which has a lot of history behind it. It is the home of the 18th President of the United States, Ulysses S. Grant, who was also a civil war general, and eight other Civil War generals – Augustus Louis Chetlain, John Oliver Duer, Jasper Adalmorn Maltby, Ely Samuel Parker, John Aaron Rawlins, William Rueben Rowley, John Corson Smith, and John Eugene Smith. Galena also boasts the oldest operating hotel in Illinois, the DeSoto House Hotel as well as numerous sites listed on the National Register of Historic Places. [119]

Leaving Galena, I was able to experience some little twisties in Illinois on the two-lane section of US 20 and stopped for a couple of scenic views of the valley along there. The sky was full of clouds, but none of them threatening, a few with dark bottoms, but mostly white puffies. Riding along I took in the farmland of Illinois, which looks a lot like the farmland of some of the other states with the usual corn, beans or wheat growing abundantly. That and getting behind another box, of course. Then there was another US 20 detour which I had to take, but fortunately, I was able to get to Rockford, Illinois without much delay. At Kegel Harley-Davidson® in Rockford, I was helped with my poker chips by an extremely sweet young lady, Haley, and I was able to successfully capture the photo op outside.

There sure was a lot of farming going on in that area east of Rockford with a lot of grain bins, lifts and so forth and then I moved through some more construction (I could not seem to get away from it). Not only that, but I was also behind a box. Anyway, I got closer to Chicago after moving out of the Rockford area and closer to the railways of Chicago. Chicago, being a big hub for air transportation and shipping and so forth is also an old railroad hub as well. Rolling into the area, there were several overpasses for train trestles over the road from their various railroad companies. Of course, I got behind another box in that area and I headed down to an area called Countryside, Illinois. [120]

There were two reasons for targeting Countryside for a stop – Little Joe's and Illinois Harley-Davidson®. At Illinois Harley-Davidson®, after eating at Little Joe's, which is an excellent Italian sausage and beef restaurant, I picked out my poker chips. The young lady that helped me there was Samantha and I got a card from her and gave her one of mine. I told her she ought to look up the Ride for Kids® and she said she would, so we will see how that goes. Illinois Harley-Davidson®, in this particular location, is on a section of the world-famous Route 66 Highway. After I secured my Ride 365 photo op there at Illinois Harley-Davidson®, I spoke with a fellow outside for a long time talking about travels and what I was doing with the Ride for Kids® and I left him with a card. [121]

After the photo op, I headed East on US 20 once again and it was good getting back into Indiana closing in on Gary, Indiana. Showing my age here I remember the song that touts Gary with the repetitive lyrics, "Gary, Indiana, Gary, Indiana, Gary, Indiana, but I digress. I did tell you that I sang to myself a lot on this trip, right? There was also construction there in Gary as well and another roundabout, actually, this was a double roundabout, so I had to navigate through that. Then I saw some other bikers on the road, which is always good to see while riding the highway. Soon after that I made it to Michigan City, Indiana and I stopped in at Harley-Davidson® of Michigan City where I got my poker chips and photo op there. I met a lady there named "Tee" and she had a 17-year-old daughter that had passed away due to a brain tumor, so I gave her a Ride for Kids® card and she was going to look it up and share. Hopefully, things will get better for her family. I also got a poker chip for a fellow that works with me who is from Michigan City, just so that he would have a little souvenir from my trip.

As I headed towards New Carlisle, Indiana, there was a great deal of construction and it just kept going and going and going, but I was eventually able to get out on the open road and see the Indiana farmland. Of course, as the day went on my shadow got longer as it had been each day while heading East. This part of Indiana is also an area that the Amish are flourishing, and I passed by a horse drawn buggy that was traveling along the edge of US 20. Then I got behind another box which made it seem like I was traveling more like the Amish for a while – not fast at all. [122] [123] Angola, Indiana was a quaint little town with interesting architecture and some very notable Civil War history. [124]

The Ohio state line was crossed before the shadows got so super long and I was able to see Ohio farmland which is also much like some of the other states, but very pretty, nonetheless. The crops include corn, beans and other grains evidenced by the grain bins in the area, though it is a lot of varied agriculture there. Along the way, it was good to see another two-wheeled friend I never met riding on the road in the opposite direction.

Now, as planned, I took a little jaunt into Michigan to also claim Michigan as a state that I rode in on this trip. It is just what you do while riding, right? Riding back into Ohio, I needed to head over to Toledo following US 20 as the sun was headed down and my shadow grew longer. In Toledo, I wanted to get on the other side to Toledo Harley-Davidson® for a photo op, as well as Signature Harley-Davidson® for the same reason, since it was already past closing time. Another reason to get to the other side of Toledo was to get a little closer to Medina, Ohio where I was going to be the next morning with an old friend from high school and her family to have breakfast at their house. Right next to Signature Harley-Davidson® was a gas station where I refueled and picked up a sandwich and drink and had dinner standing next to the bike before the photo op at Signature. Then, it was time to head towards my hotel for the night in Norwalk, Ohio. A little intermittent rain was about, but not too much to worry about, so that was the way it was on Day 21.

McGrath
Dubuque
Harley-
Davidson®
photo op

Starting
out from
Dubuque
with a US
20 detour
into
Wisconsin

Crossing the Mississippi into Wisconsin

From Wisconsin Into Illinois

Galena, Illinois

Illinois Farmland

Kegel
Harley-
Davidson®
in
Rockford,
Illinois

Grain
is good

Chicago area

Railways
abound
as
Chicago
draws
near

Illinois
Harley-
Davidson®

Illinois
Harley-
Davidson®
photo op

Gary Indiana, Gary Indiana, Gary Indiana

Illinois Harley-Davidson® of Michigan City

Indiana
Farmland

The Amish
in a
mechanized
world

Angola, Indiana

Ohio State Line

My little
jaunt into
Michigan

Closing
in on
Toledo

Toledo
Harley-
Davidson®

Signature
Harley-
Davidson®

Day 22

Plan

Day	Starting Point / Ending Point	Miles / Ride Time	Potential Lodging	Potential Dining at Destination	Potential Attractions En Route
22 (Thur, July 30)	Perrysburg, OH Geneva, NY	398 10:36	Microtel Inn & Suites Geneva	Water Street Café Halsey's Restaurant The Rusty Pig	• Breakfast at hotel • Real breakfast at 0800 at Katherine's Family Restaurant, Cleveland, OH with the Links (Dine-In); • Lunch at Kardohely's Family Restaurant, Ashtabula, OH (Take-out); • H-D of Erie, Erie, PA; • Geneva H-D, Geneva, NY; (if before 1800)

Actual

Day	Starting Point / Ending Point	Miles / Ride Time	Lodging	Dining at Destination	Attractions En Route
22 (Thur, July 30)	Norwalk, OH Geneva, NY	398 10:36	Microtel Inn & Suites Geneva		• Light breakfast at hotel • Real breakfast at 0800 at the Links' home (Dine-In) Medina, OH; • Stinger H-D, Medina, OH; • Lunch at Mallorca Restaurant, Cleveland, OH (Dine-In); • Gas stop in Wickliffe, OH; • Gas stop in Fredonia, NY; • Laundry at hotel

Leaving out of Norwalk, going into Medina I had to get off the road a little bit, so I had to come back to that point to continue with US 20 headed East. I did go down into Medina had a great visit with Vicki and Gary Link and their family (daughter and granddaughter) who lived with them at that time, but have since moved out, so they have become empty nesters. Vicki used to work at the Harley-Davidson® dealership in Medina as well as the one back in Winchester Virginia, where we went to high school. She came back to Winchester to work there because a friend of hers owned that particular one, Groves Winchester Harley-Davidson®. Neither she nor Gary ride anymore though. After a wonderful breakfast at the Link's, I stopped at the Stinger Harley-Davidson® in Medina, picked out my T-shirt, poker chips and then did my photo op there. I then headed out to get back to US 20 and, of course, construction - even on the back roads. It was a partly cloudy day that morning and not a whole lot of sunshine at first, but it was still a good day to be riding.

Reaching US 20 again, I headed up to Cleveland and on US 20, of course, there is construction around there as well through which I had to navigate, but I did find a classic restaurant called the Mallorca like the

Spanish island. It was a Spanish lunch and, boy was it a lot of food! I got the "Pechuga de Pollo en Salsa de Ajo", which is Chicken in Garlic Sauce. It was a good lunch, but I could not eat it all, so I ate the really good stuff and left some of their extra carbs and bread on the plate. [125]

US 20 travels through Cleveland on Euclid Avenue where the very first electric traffic light was installed back in 1914, so there is some interesting history about it that I learned after the fact. I know from experience that there are a whole lot more traffic lights in Cleveland now on US 20. [126] It seems I stopped at every one as I tried to cross town and it seemed like forever and a day to get through town.

Then you travel for, it seems like for miles, and you do not see any signage to tell you that you are on the road you think you are on you can get a little concerned about just where you are. Then there was more construction as well to confuse the situation. Finally, some signage appeared for US 20. I cannot count the times when I have either made a turn or crossed an intersection and gone for what seems like miles before I can confirm that the road I was on was really the one I had expected. East of Cleveland I rode into Conneaut, the last Ohio town on this trip, before getting into Pennsylvania. [127]

My goal was to get to Geneva, New York for the night because I had a hotel reservation there and it was just necessary to get that far, so I had to pass up some other stops along the way, even Harley-Davidson® of Erie, Pennsylvania. I rode through Girard, Pennsylvania, which was an old town with some well-crafted buildings with ornate carvings as well as statuary in the streets. [128] [129] It was almost a ride back in time.

When riding on US 20 through Pennsylvania, it was good to see other bikers out and about and, of course, I always welcome the waves. Then I rode into New York and seeing the New York farmland was again, much the same as many of the rest of the states, which some people do not believe is possible. It is definitely a reality as I can report from first-hand knowledge having ridden through the New York countryside before and there is definitely some beautiful farmland in many places in New York State. New York City, you can forget about, in my humble opinion, but New York State has been blessed with a lot of beautiful farmland.

The little town of Ripley was displaying United States flags as were many little towns along the way. I am not sure if it was because of the short time frame after the July 4th Independence Day celebrations that they were still up or they left them there most of the time, but there were a lot of towns that had flags displayed on light poles and power poles along the route. In Ripley, I passed by some bikes parked at an establishment, but did not have the time to stop and check them out. [130]

At this point on the trip, the weather was still lots of sunshine, blue skies and white wispies and I was thankful for that. Rolling into Westfield, New York, I saw several downtown buildings that were very much old school architecture and was intrigued enough to research a little after I made it home. There is an interesting story about Westfield, which was about Grace Bedell and her relationship to Abraham Lincoln. Westfield, New York was home of Grace Bedell, who was not known to the author until some post trip research uncovered an interesting fact. [131] It is a fairly good legend for the nice little town of Westfield and there were more flags on street signs, power poles and other appurtenances as well.

Brocton, New York was the same way with the flags on display. They also have an interesting Town Center where they have 2 semi-circular arches that crossed the road from one corner to the other like two crisscrossing rainbows that held up the "Brocton" sign, and it was remarkably interesting. [132]

Vineyards were evident along this stretch of US 20 as I rode into Silver Creek, New York. Too bad I did not get a chance to stop and stock up, but as I said before, I had a mission to get to Geneva. Those shadows kept getting longer and the last picture of the day was near Orchard Park, New York as the sunset was very pretty, but it was the last time I could take a picture with the dash cam and have it turn out without much light. [133]

I will not tell you what time I rolled into Geneva, New York for the night, but it was about 140 miles from Silver Creek where I had mentioned the sun was going down in the West. It was a good bit later than dark-thirty; however, I was able to sleep after doing much needed laundry in the hotel.

Stinger
Harley-
Davidson®

Stinger
Harley-
Davidson®
photo op

Entering
Cleveland

Lunch at
the
Mallorca
Restaurant

The long way of US 20 in Cleveland

Finally some signage appears

Conneaut,
the last
Ohio
town on
this trip

Pennsylvania
State Line

Girard,
Pennsylvania

The
Town
of
North
East

New York
Farmland

Ripley,
New
York

New York
Vineyards

Westfield,
New York

Brocton,
New York

Silver
Creek,
New
York

Day 23

Plan

Day	Starting Point / Ending Point	Miles / Ride Time	Potential Lodging	Potential Dining at Destination	Potential Attractions En Route
23 (Fri, July 31)	Geneva, NY Southborough, MA	391 9:58	Red Roof Inn Boston - Southborough/ Worcester	Harry's Restaurant (Take-out); Chick-fil-A (Take-out)	• Breakfast at Water Street Café, Geneva (Take-out); • Harriet Tubman National Historical Park, Auburn, NY (prior to opening); • Lorenzo State Historic Site, Cazenovia, NY; • Lunch at Chicken Joe's Albany, Albany, NY (Take-out); • Sheldon's H-D, Auburn, MA; • US 20 Endpoint at Boston Buckminster Hotel (at Brookline Street) • (Laundry Day – Westboro Laundromat, 164 Milk St, Westborough, MA 01581)

Actual

Day	Starting Point / Ending Point	Miles / Ride Time	Lodging	Dining at Destination	Attractions En Route
23 (Fri, July 31)	Geneva, NY Old Sturbridge Village, MA	391 9:58	Old Sturbridge Inn & Reeder Family Lodges	Old Sturbridge Pizza & Restaurant	• Geneva H-D, Geneva, NY; • Gas up in Geneva, NY; • City of Geneva Information Center (Post cards); • Post Office; • Historical Park, Auburn, NY (Rode by prior to opening); • Lorenzo State Historic Site, Cazenovia, NY (Rode by); • Lunch at Dave's Diner, Cazenovia, NY (Dine-In); • Gas stop at Pittsfield, MA; • Supper from Old Sturbridge Pizza & Restaurant

After a late night at the hotel in Geneva, New York where I did laundry and all that sort of good stuff into the wee hours of the morning, I just said I was going to have a late start that day, so I went to Geneva Harley-Davidson® for my photo op and poker chips there. After that I rode around Geneva for little bit to see the sights and get some photos as well as mail some post cards after picking them up at the visitor center on the lake. So, I thought I would have a look and it was really quite fascinating in downtown Geneva. [134] [135]

The next little town along US 20 was Waterloo, New York, and there is a story about that nice old town reflected in the back of the book. [136] [137] [138]

Then Seneca Falls, New York was the next town in line and there is some interesting history for the town as well. It is said that this town is the scene for Bedford Falls of the "It's a Wonderful Life" movie with Jimmy Stewart, so that is what they say. [139] [140]

The New York farmland, like I said before, was particularly picturesque scenery as there are wonderfully working farms just like many other states I went through on this trip. I saw blue skies and white puffy clouds still in abundance as I rode into Auburn, New York. US 20 passes to the rear of St. Mary's Church, which was created when the bishop split the Catholics of the town of Auburn and made two parishes from the Catholics of Holy Family parish. [141]

The Underground Railroad passed through Auburn in the 1850's and was later home for one of its founders, Harriett Tubman. The Harriett Tubman Home was off to the right or South, but I had to make tracks to get as close to Boston as I could before the end of the day, so a planned visit had to be scrubbed. It was a pity that I did not get to go to Harriet Tubman's home near Highway 20, but it was just a little bit off the road and I really was intent on getting as close to Boston and then down to Harrisburg, Pennsylvania the next day, so I did not take too many side trips on Day 23. [142] [143]

After Auburn I went through Skaneateles, New York and it was much like the other towns of the Finger Lakes region. Welch Allyn, Inc. Corporate Headquarters is located there and is a producer of medical equipment including defibrillators, patient monitoring devices, thermometry devices, etc. The company is the largest employer in the town. An interesting little tidbit (I thought) about an otherwise tourist town on a lake. The countryside was just aglow this beautiful sunny day with a few clouds, but mostly sunny. It has been said that the town's population doubles during July and August due to the combination of residents coming back home from winter respites in Florida and tourists renting cottages along the lakefront for the summer.

Riding over toward Lafayette, New York, brought me back to my youth growing up near Winchester, Virginia. Why, you ask? Just so you know it seemed remarkably similar to Winchester because US Highway 11 and Interstate 81 both run through or near Winchester, yet there they were, way up in Lafayette, New York. Those were roads I traveled from the Winchester area where I went to high school down to Virginia Tech when I was going back and forth that 4-hour trip to go to school. When attending Virginia Tech in the 70's, I made many trips up and down both roads. When I-81 became snarled or snowbound, US 11 provided an alternative route and vice-versa. Crossing them both here in the Lafayette, New York area was both different and familiar, and somewhat nostalgic.

US 11 may become one of my bucket list end-to-end US Highway rides, but that remains to be seen. It travels from Rouses Point, New York about 240 miles to the north of Lafayette, down to Bayou Sauvage (New Orleans), Louisiana over 1350 miles to the south. Someday, maybe….

I knew I was not going to make it to Boston that night, so I planned on stopping short and making up time in the morning to be able to still get to Harrisburg, Pennsylvania in time for Susquehanna Valley Harley-Davidson® the next day. It had been great weather that day, so I thought I should be able to make some time and see how it would go. At that point, I did not know where I would end up as I cancelled the reservation in Boston, so I had to end up somewhere. Hopefully, there would be a place available before the weather and the darkness made riding through the mountains less than desirable.

New York agriculture is not normally what one thinks about when someone mentions "New York" in conversations, but, while I already knew that firsthand from previous travels through the state*, this trip provided even more beautiful evidence of that fact. There were cornfields galore along US 20 for several long stretches in New York.

*Previously completed US Highway sections in New York include US 15, US 209, US 219, as well as the Sunrise Highway (NY27) and NY25 (Main Road) to Orient Point to catch the Cross Sound Ferry over to New London, Connecticut. Probably most of us do not really know about how much Long Island is a thriving agricultural area, but it definitely was along NY25 and NY27.

It was always a glad sight to meet other bikers on the road, even though we may never speak to one another in person. I kept meeting them almost everywhere, so there is a whole bunch of folks out there that are "friends I haven't met" yet. And then, I got behind another box, but this time had a passing lane on my side.

Cazenovia, New York, is a town on Cazenovia Lake, which is approximately 10 miles around and 45 feet deep. [144] Following another biker into Cazenovia, which is a quaint little town, it became rather hot as I recall, so I was glad to find a spot to stop. Well, it was about two o'clock, a little after that really, and I was in Cazenovia, so I stopped at Dave's Diner [145] to have lunch. That was a no-brainer, right? I asked the young lady, Alexis, who was serving me, what her favorite lunch item was, and she told me something that was not on the menu. And I said, "I'll have one of those." It was a big wrap, and I also added coleslaw and what they call salt potatoes. The name of the wrap that Alexis recommended was the "Club Royale." All the folks there were genuinely nice and served up a great lunch. The town is also home to Cazenovia College, a small liberal arts school with around 865 students, give or take. [146]

US 20, for at least a section, is a New York scenic byway and then I found myself riding through the village of Morrisville, New York. [147] While there, I got to see some more bikers riding through to the West. Wouldn't you know, there was also construction, even in the New York farmland? I guess that is to be expected during the summer months everywhere.

In Richfield Springs, New York, US flags were flying on the poles along the street as I had seen in many towns during my travels. Good to see the patriotism in so many places. [148] The town of Richfield Springs is located near Canadarago Lake to the south and is also included in the Official Cooperstown website as a stopping point before going to the town where baseball was born. [149] I did not have enough time in the day's schedule to pop down to Cooperstown about 15 miles south at the southern end of Otsego Lake, but I sure would have loved to spend some time at the Hall of Fame. Baseball has been one of my favorite sports to follow growing up, possibly because my father played in college and in the Army as well as playing myself in my younger days.

Two railroads crisscross US 20 near Fullers, New York, a sight rarely seen by these old eyes of mine, or for that matter very few others. It is referred to as a flyover when one track "flies" over another, but this one is where one track flies over another and they both fly over a US highway. Check out some of the discussion

I found on a railroad blog at the link in the back of the book. [150]

As I rode through Albany, New York, I recalled another Albany on US 20 that I also rode through several days previously. One Albany on this trip was on US 20 farther West back out in Oregon and there is the Albany in New York on the eastern part of US 20. The Cathedral of the Immaculate Conception is right on US 20 in Albany, New York, and I was glad to capture a photo as I rode by. [151]

Somewhere along one of the two-lane sections of US 20 I found myself in Massachusetts and that section of US 20 was part of the Lafayette Trail. General Lafayette embarked on what would be called today as a farewell tour after the Revolutionary War and sections of highways are marked to indicate his travel route. [152]

My shadow was getting longer as I was riding into Pittsfield, Massachusetts and I still could not get away from construction. It is just all over the place. Lee, Massachusetts was supposedly the gateway to the Berkshires, and it was interesting to read up on that. [153] Lee, Massachusetts is often referred to as the "gateway to the Berkshires" and provides tourists a quaint place to stay while planning and conducting excursions into the mountains. The Berkshires are an extremely popular destination for quiet, scenic countryside vacations and tends to cater to the New York to Boston crowd, being almost equidistant from both.

The Historic US Route 20 Visitor Center is in Chester, Massachusetts right on US 20. I did not have time to stop, but later learned of the effort of Bryan Farr and others to document the history of the highway and establishing the Historic Route 20 Association in 2012. I purchased his book, "HISTORIC US ROUTE 20: A JOURNEY ACROSS AMERICA'S LONGEST HIGHWAY", which has a lot of good information about it with many color photos inside. His book has a lot of photos and captions describing what his experience was traveling the highway, but I did not know that until later. Of course, it was closed by the time I arrived, and it was getting later, so I had to keep moving. [154]

I rode into Huntington, Massachusetts and was impressed yet again with the many US flags flying along the street. Our country is a true gift from God, and it is heartwarming to see such a display of patriotism. [155] After leaving Huntington, I rode through several towns in the hills while covering the last fifty or sixty miles for the day including Westfield, West Springfield, Ludlow, Palmer, Brimfield until finally reaching the Old Sturbridge Inn & Reeder Family Lodges, in Old Sturbridge Village as darkness set in.

Not having eaten any dinner, because I was trying to get as far East as I could before it became dark in the hills, the innkeeper pointed me to a pizza place down the street. I called before they closed, ordered a pizza, walked down to the convenience store next to the pizza place, picked up a beer and then picked up my pizza. I brought it back to the room and had pizza and beer for the night then had a good night's sleep. The next morning it would be cold pizza for breakfast.

Geneva
Harley-
Davidson®
photo op

Geneva,
New
York

Waterloo, New York

Seneca Falls, New York

Auburn, New York

New York Cornfields

Entering
Cazenovia,
New York

Village of
Morrisville,
New York

Richfield
Springs,
New York

Two
railroads
crisscross
US 20
near
Fullers,
New
York

Cathedral of the Immaculate Conception in Albany, NY

General Lafayette Trail on US 20 in Massachusetts

Entering
Pittsfield,
Massachusetts

Lee,
Massachusetts
is often
referred to as
the "Gateway
to the
Berkshires"

Historic
US Route
20 Visitor
Center
Chester,
MA

Huntington,
MA

Plan

Day	Starting Point / Ending Point	Miles / Ride Time	Potential Lodging	Potential Dining at Destination	Potential Attractions En Route
24 (Sat, Aug. 1)	Southborough, MA Harrisburg, PA	373 5:46	Ramada Inn Harrisburg/ Hershey	Grill 22; Brother Joe's Pizza	• Breakfast at Honey Dew Donuts (Take-out); • H-D of Danbury, Danbury, CT; • Williams H-D, Lebanon, NJ (Optional per time); • Battlefield H-D, Gettysburg, PA (Optional per time); • Susquehanna Valley H-D, Harrisburg, PA; • 1700 Mass at Holy Name of Jesus, Harrisburg, PA

Actual

Day	Starting Point / Ending Point	Miles / Ride Time	Lodging	Dining at Destination	Attractions En Route
24 (Sat, Aug. 1)	Old Sturbridge Village, MA Harrisburg, PA	373 5:46	Ramada Inn Harrisburg/ Hershey	Mikado's	• Breakfast leftover from Old Sturbridge Pizza & Restaurant; • US 20 Endpoint at Boston Buckminster Hotel (at Brookline Street); • Gas on I-90 Service Center, Charlton, MA; • Gas stop at Lake Ariel, PA; • Susquehanna Valley H-D, Harrisburg, PA; • Supper at Mikado's

A cold pizza breakfast turned out to be surprisingly good, mostly due to the great pizza I bought the night before. You do what you have to do, right? Anyway, having adequately filled my belly with tasty pizza, I left out of Old Sturbridge Village. As I came out of the hills from the village, I rode through Charlton, Massachusetts.

I did a little research digging around after the trip and found a little tidbit of nostalgia about a famous cane that was sent to 700 towns in New England by the Boston Post, of which Charlton was one. It turns out that the cane for the town of Charlton has been missing and there is an appeal for the townspeople to search for it. [156]

The next town in the string of towns along the Massachusetts portion of US 20 route was Oxford, with just a little tidbit of history I uncovered after the trip and is found in the back of the book for those history buffs (like me) to review as interest is piqued. [157] The string of towns continued with Worcester and in case you have not noticed by now, I do like to learn about the places through which I travel, so if I did not research it beforehand, I did so afterwards. [158] [159]

Shrewsbury was next up for Massachusetts towns along US 20. I did not have any previous knowledge of Shrewsbury, but I have some friends whose last name is Shrewsbury, so I thought it was interesting to see a town in Massachusetts of the same name. I did a little post trip research and found some intriguing information (to me anyway). [160]

Heading along toward Boston, I rode through Northborough, which I thought was a genuinely nice old town with a number of houses along the road. [161] Riding along Williams Lake, I observed the area and enjoyed the view as I headed toward Wayland. [162]

Riding through Waltham, Massachusetts I was reminded of my childhood once again because when I was very young, I was given a Waltham wristwatch by my parents. I wore it until I learned my skin attacked any metal parts in contact with it, so I had to stop wearing any type of watch or jewelry on my person. Some of you may know about Waltham watches and some of you may not, so there are other little tidbits in the back of the book. [163] [164]

Soon after the Waltham area, I reached Boston and the endpoint of US 20, did the ride by and U-Turn to capture the photo of the sign you see when looking West which says that Newport, Oregon is 3365 miles away. After that photo op, I was able to see the Boston Hotel Buckminster [165], which is where I had planned to stay, at one point in in in the planning stages. I had to forego that because I was by myself and did not really care to be in downtown Boston overnight. I had also planned to stay a little further south, but as it was, I did not make it to that point the night before as planned. I was planning to be past Boston and in the Southborough area, but I stopped in Old Sturbridge Village to not push on during the night in the mountains (and dark). My goal for this day was to get to Harrisburg, Pennsylvania for the night and to be able to get to Susquehanna Valley Harley-Davidson® before they closed.

After the Boston US 20 end point, I was just going to make tracks to Harrisburg, so I had to backtrack on US 20 to be able to get up on I-90 to head West again. I went through Connecticut and some lovely scenery along the way even though it was Interstate. I do not like riding Interstates as a rule, but it was the only way to get there fast, so I had to do it this time. I went through Hartford, Connecticut, and it was nice getting to travel with the bright blue sky above me. I do not know how or why, but I had the same kind of light show under the overpass there in Hartford as I did in the Buffalo Bill Reservoir Tunnel back in Wyoming. I guess I will have to find out about that phenomenon someday, but for now, I do not have an explanation other than electromagnetic light diffraction (just kidding).

Riding into Hartford (we learned back in elementary school was the capital of Connecticut) was somewhat fascinating to see, but some may or may not know a little about some interesting facts about Hartford. Some of which are found in the back of the book. [166] [167] [168]

Moving past Hartford, Connecticut into New York State again, Honness Mountain became visible in the distance as I gazed into the New York countryside. I noticed there were flags on several of the overpasses that crossed the Interstate and that was always a good sight to see. Once in New York, I motored to the Hudson River and crossed it on the "Hamilton Fish" Newburgh-Beacon Bridge. [169]

The Delaware River separates New York and Pennsylvania and I crossed into Pennsylvania at the Port Jervis / Matamoras area. Of course, I ended up with construction on the road, even on the Interstate. As I got closer to Harrisburg, Pennsylvania, or to the turn off for Harrisburg near the Scranton - Wilkes-Barre, Pennsylvania area where I-84 and I-81 intersect to head South to Harrisburg, I recalled the last time I crossed I-81 was up in Lafayette, New York. I then found myself back on I-81 headed South towards Harrisburg. Interstate 81 is still one of my favorite interstates as far as mountain and valley scenery goes, even in Pennsylvania, but in Virginia I-81 runs right through the Shenandoah Valley which is just a beautiful Interstate as interstates go. If you must travel Interstate, that is a good one to take and again, I was trying to make tracks, so there were not very many stops except for gas.

As I approached Harrisburg, the clouds started forming and seemed threatening, but it really was not any precipitation flying around, so I did not hit any bad weather all the way down to Susquehanna Valley Harley-Davidson®. I was hoping I could meet the person there with whom I had made contact originally who was so excited about my trip and the Ride for Kids® that she even made a donation. Too bad she was not working that day so I could not say "Hi" to Emily, but at least I was able to get my shirt and my poker chips there. I did also manage to get my photo op as well. At the end of the day, I was successful making my goal and I was able to talk with the great folks at Susquehanna, buy a Tee-shirt and poker chips just before closing time, so it was a good day all in all.

For the life of me, I cannot remember where I "went" to Mass, but I know I did online somewhere that evening. I just did not record it anywhere, I guess. That is just part of the aging process, you start to forget......

Riding
through
Charlton,
MA

Oxford,
MA

Worcester, MA

Shrewsbury, MA

The Town of
Northborough

Williams
Lake

Entering
Wayland,
MA

Waltham,
MA

Did the turnabout to catch the westward sign for Newport, Oregon

The landmark Boston Hotel Buckminster

Now
Taking the
Interstate
into
Connecticut

Riding
into
Hartford

Light
show
under
the
overpass

Loving
the
Flags

Crossing
the
Hudson
River on
Hamilton
Fish
Bridge

Pennsylvania
State Line

Hoping to get to Susquehanna Harley-Davidson® before the rain

Susquehanna Harley-Davidson® photo op

Plan

Day	Starting Point / Ending Point	Miles / Ride Time	Potential Lodging	Potential Dining at Destination	Potential Attractions En Route
25 (Sun, Aug. 2)	Harrisburg, PA Rocky Mount, NC	381 8:49	Quality Inn; Country Inn & Suites; Holiday Inn; Candlewood Suites	The Highway Diner; LouReda's; An American Table; Highway 55; Cracker Barrel;	• Dunkin (0600 Sunday Breakfast) (Take-out); • Gas up at Jock's Exxon, Leesburg, VA; • Old Dominion H-D, Fredericksburg, VA; • Lunch at Hardee's, Ashland, VA with Paul & Lynn Muller; • Gas up in Ashland, VA; • Richmond H-D, Ashland, VA (Optional per time); • Black Cat H-D, Rocky Mount, NC (If before 1700)

Actual

Day	Starting Point / Ending Point	Miles / Ride Time	Lodging	Dining at Destination	Attractions En Route
25 (Sun, Aug. 2)	Harrisburg, PA Rocky Mount, NC	381 8:49	Candlewood Suites	The Highway Diner	• Breakfast at Sheetz, Thurmont, MD (Take-out); • Gas up at Sheetz, Thurmont, MD; • Lunch at Hardee's, Ashland, VA after visit with Paul & Lynn Muller (Take-out); • Gas up at WAWA in Ashland, VA; • Richmond H-D, Ashland, VA; • Black Cat H-D, Rocky Mount, NC (Photo op only); • Supper at Highway Diner (Dine-In)

Heading out of Harrisburg, Pennsylvania, the little bit of bad weather had gone through the night before with a little rain and so forth and there were still a few lingering clouds, but there was a blue sky behind them, so it was not so bad. As it turned out, I did not need to have rain gear on, but I decided to put it on just because it looked like it might be something down the road. Not too far down the road, it became apparent that rain gear was not necessary, so as I rode into Maryland and found a place to stop for gas and breakfast it had to come off. I had a breakfast sandwich and some coffee at the Sheetz gas station in Thurmont, Maryland. This day was the day I was going to complete riding US 15 end-to-end by completing the section from Harrisburg, Pennsylvania down to Leesburg, Virginia, so I was traveling South on US 15.

Going through Maryland, clouds started to dissipate as I approached Frederick where it was more of a sunny, cloudy, partly cloudy, partly sunny day down there, so it was a pleasant ride. Riding through Frederick on US 15 South, I continued on and saw some signs which indicated Leesburg, Virginia was the right direction, which was reassuring. I also rode through some construction, of course. As always, it was good to see some other bikers along Route 15 and then I negotiated another roundabout while I was still in Maryland.

I crossed the Potomac into Virginia and some bikers that I encountered were headed the other direction, so that was good to experience the mutual wave once more. In Virginia, of course, they have their slogan "Virginia is for Lovers" that they have used for many, many years. I was glad I was on that road after the rain instead of riding through it and that particular road was a nice tree-lined two-lane road, which was most enjoyable. As I said, I never get enough of seeing other bikers on the road and within just a few miles into Virginia, I met at least 4 others in as many miles and enjoyed giving them the biker wave.

My birth state of Virginia also has wine country, which was enlightening as I did not experience that in any areas where I lived while growing up. They may have blossomed more after I moved from the state and I would not know since I did not travel through this specific area very much over the last 30 years.

Following US 15 down to Leesburg, Virginia I was able to claim victory on completing US 15 end-to-end, and, of course, I had to get into some construction while I was there so you can never miss that, can you? After making Leesburg, I continued South on US 15 to get down to US 17 where I was going to head south from that intersection down to Port Royal again to complete that northern little bit of US 17. Farther down US 17, the clouds started getting a little thick again, blocking the sun a little, but it did not rain on me and then I got behind another box as I approached Port Royal. From there, I would end up riding down US 301, so I completed my northern section of US 17 and then prepared for the long trip down US 301 to complete another end-to-end section of a US highway.

As I was heading South on US 301, the clouds dissipated for good and I started to see blue skies and just green growth everywhere, from the grass to the trees to everything that was growing. US 301 parallels Interstate 95 for a lot of the length of it in Virginia as well as North Carolina, but it is definitely a lot more peaceful ride. You may not go as fast, but in a lot of ways it is a lot more relaxing on the two-lane road because the traffic is almost non-existent, so you get to see the local fields and crops and trees up close. Then, I closed in on Virginia State Route 54 where I was going to ride over to Ashland, Virginia to meet up with an old college buddy and his wife and possibly have lunch with them.

I spent a lot of time in Ashland growing up because my father's parents lived there in the house that my grandfather built. I do not really know when he built it because it was the only house that I remember them living in while I was growing up, so I really had to ride by there on this trip. It is on the corner of Louisiana and College Avenues behind what used to be the Luck Motor Company, which was on US Highway 1. The auto dealer was just behind the house there, but that went away, and it is now a Hardee's right behind their old house. My grandmother survived my grandfather for many years, but she passed away almost twenty years ago. My father had to sell their house, so that was hard, but it was necessary, and it is a prime property if anybody ever wanted to do something else with it. I reveled in a bit of nostalgia while riding by there.

Also, in Ashland is Randolph Macon College where my father went to school. That was where he played baseball and football, but mostly his claim to fame there was baseball. I think he ended up with a batting average of over 400. He would do everything with his right hand except swing, so he was a left-handed hitter and was able to hit a good many home runs in his college career. He went into the Army and continued to play baseball for the Army while he was stationed in Kobe Japan. The story behind that is that he went over there in the Army and was teaching chemical and biological warfare while also playing baseball. The Japanese, at that time in the 50's, and still today, really love the sport of baseball.

How it worked out for my father and mother was my father was over there and he sent back home for my mother. No, they had not been married yet, but he sent for her to come over and they would get married. So, she did, and the way it was then, they had to get married by the American Consulate as well as a Japanese representative, so they were married twice. As it turns out, when speaking at my mother's funeral, a few years ago, I mentioned a lot of things I had at that time were made in Japan. I said my car was made in Japan, my guitar was made in Japan, my motorcycle at that time was made in Japan, even I was made in Japan! I was born in Richmond, Virginia, but I was "Made in Japan". That is a whole other story about how my mother came home with me inside and not telling anybody until she got to her parent's house, took off her coat and revealed the obvious. They all raved over it, but I digress.

I had a nice visit there with my friend Paul Muller and his wife, Lynn. We sat around on the campus there on the Adirondack chairs that the college had set out under the trees and, of course, at this point we had to do the social distancing thing because of the COVID-19. Then, after that nice visit, I did eat lunch at the Hardee's behind my grandparent's old house, while standing beside the bike.

After lunch, I made it to Richmond Harley-Davidson® for my poker chips and photo op. I had already been there before and had a T-shirt, so I did not need another one, but Richmond Harley-Davidson® is right there near Ashland, so that was an easy stop at that point. Then I rode back up to catch US 301 where I had left it and started back heading South toward the City of Richmond.

There was a little bit of rain starting, but nothing much, so I went through Richmond down US 301, which follows Chamberlayne Avenue through the city. As I mentioned before, I was born in Richmond, Virginia at the Medical College of Virginia way back in 1955. While US 301 travels down Chamberlayne Avenue, a few streets over is Monument Avenue where there are/were many statues from Richmond history, many from the Civil War. If you have not figured it out by now, I really like learning about the history of places I visit or have resided. [170]

Richmond has a lot of history, but one of the things I remember personally experiencing was the annual Thanksgiving parade and football game sometimes between Virginia Tech and University of Virginia for the Tobacco Bowl. Richmond was the home of Philip Morris, a tobacco company noted for cigarette manufacturing, and I remember the famous "Call for Philip Morris" from the diminutive "Johnny", the bell hop from a convertible in the parade. [171]

Another thing I remember while growing up in Richmond is the Richmond Braves Baseball team and watching the games at Parker Field. We used to drive down Chamberlayne Avenue to the area of the ballpark. The Richmond team was the International League (AAA) farm team of the Atlanta Braves and former Atlanta Braves dugout coach, Jim Beauchamp, was a player when I watched the Richmond Braves play. [172] [173]

Crossing the Appomattox River, I rode into Petersburg, a town which also has a long history. [174] Remember I mentioned some time before about losing signage as you cross intersections or make turns?

Well, after I crossed the Appomattox River into Petersburg, there was a sign that indicated US 301 turned to the left at the next intersection. Upon making the turn, I asked myself, "OK, is 301 really this way?" It just did not look like it was really a US highway as it appeared to be a back street, so I thought, "No way, US 301 Really?" Yep, it was, but I must admit, I did a few U-turns and block circling before charging down the road that would ultimately prove to be US 301. I had to make another turn at an intersection but that was the road that led you back to US 301. The other thing is that once you get on a highway where you do not really have a whole lot of signage on the road, you must wait until there is an intersection and look sideways to see if it still says it is even the road you want (US 301 in this case).

Again, construction plagued me, even on that little part of the highway, but US 301 is still a relaxing alternative to I-95. I specifically wanted to be on US 301 to claim that section of highway that I was wanting to ride end to end on my bucket list, and I pretty much had the route to myself most of the time. There were times where it was right next to I-95 and I could see the traffic over there and see the almost nonexistent traffic on US 301 where I was riding.

I was riding into North Carolina with virtually no one else on the road and it was pretty interesting when reviewing some of the dash cam photos that I got of that stretch. It was just hardly anybody on the road going either direction, but I got to see the North Carolina farmland, where there was corn, tobacco, soybeans, and lots of various crops there. At one point, it was just me and the tar snakes on the road.

I did make it to Black Cat Harley-Davidson® for my Ride 365 photograph, but not in time for collecting poker chips there in Rocky Mount, North Carolina. I checked into the Candlewood Suites which is next to the Highway Diner which was next to the Black Cat Harley-Davidson® dealership. They are all literally within walking distance sharing the same driveway and parking lot area. So where was I going to have dinner? The Highway Diner, of course. The dinner was awesome. The server that helped me was Genese, and she was genuinely nice and thoughtful, and I appreciated her service.

Back in the room after an exceptionally fine dinner, I did the nightly recharging and uploading routine in preparation for the final day of the ride home.

Heading
into
Maryland
and
potential
weather

Completing
the last part
of US 15
for another
bucket list
item

Crossing
the
Potomac

Virginia
is for
Lovers

Virginia
Wine
Country

Leesburg
completes
US 15 for
me

Northern
section
of US 17
complete
and now
for US
301

Love
the
solitude
of US
301

The house my grandfather built

Richmond
Harley-
Davidson®

Richmond
Harley-
Davidson®
photo op

US 301 in Richmond

Crossing the James River

Appomattox
River at
Petersburg

US 301 is
the
relaxing
alternative
to I-95

US 301
into
North
Carolina

Just me
and the
tar
snakes
and a
rare
sight,
another
vehicle

North
Carolina
Farmland

Black Cat
Harley-
Davidson®
photo op

Day 26

Plan

Day	Starting Point / Ending Point	Miles / Ride Time	Potential Lodging	Potential Dining at Destination	Potential Attractions En Route
26 (Mon, Aug. 3)	Rocky Mount, NC Home	358 7:48	Home	Home	• Breakfast at Chew N Chat Café (Take-out); • Lunch at Village Station 1893 Restaurant, Lumberton, NC (Take-out); • Gas up at Shell, 5030 Fayetteville Rd, Lumberton, NC; • Gas up at Fuel 24 in Manning, SC; • Summerton, SC; • Thunder Tower H-D, Columbia, SC

Actual

Day	Starting Point / Ending Point	Miles / Ride Time	Lodging	Dining at Destination	Attractions En Route
26 (Mon, Aug. 3)	Rocky Mount, NC Home	358 7:48	Home	Home	• Breakfast at Highway Diner (Dine-In); • Gas up in Smithfield, NC; • Gas up in Lumberton, NC; • Sandwich lunch at Shell station, Lumberton, NC (Take-out); • Gas up in Manning, SC; • Summerton, SC to complete northern section of US 301; • Back roads to I-20 to Home

The last day on the way home opened after an overnight rain with just a little misty spit around, but my breakfast was awesome. They call it the U-turn breakfast at the Highway Diner. My server was Marshall, and he was a really good guy. We chatted a good bit, and I gave him a Ride for Kids® card and told them what I was doing on my cross-country ride. He was so excited about it, he said, 'I'm gonna share this with a friend of mine. He's got a lot more people that follow him on social media, so it will get it out there and get some information out so that folks know." And he was all excited and then the time came for paying my bill and he says that he had it covered. I said, "What?" He said, "Yep, I've got it covered, don't worry about it." So, hats off to the folks there at the Highway Diner and Marshall that morning. The night before my server was Genese, and she was an excellent server and hopefully, I will get around there again sometime.

When leaving Rocky Mount, the question that came up in my mind looking ahead was, "Am I going to be wet or am I going be dry?" Just based on the clouds hanging around, I also asked myself "Do I put rain gear on or not?" I chose not and it was the best choice because the clouds did not do much and did not last long and I got into some sunshine by the time I got to Micro, North Carolina. I was enjoying the white wispies and the blue skies there as well as all the different crops riding along with corn, tobacco, soybeans, and other grains. Then, I started to look ahead, and it looked like riding in the rain was going to be inevitable. It looked like it was just going to be a short shower, so I tucked my socks down into my boots and kept on going. I did get wet, but the inside of my boots and socks did not, so I got through that little stretch of rain and back to where it was just white wispy clouds and some blue skies again. [175] That was in the little town of Dunn, North Carolina when I ran through the shower.

After that, I noticed some dark skies up ahead across the Cape Fear River and the same type of thing as before, semi-overcast skies and the impression of potential rainy weather, as I approached Fayetteville, North Carolina. I still rode through some construction in that particular area near Fayetteville, though. [176]

I remember "South of the Border" as a kid and it seems like it has been there forever. South of the Border is a Mexican theme park in South Carolina just South of the state line between North Carolina and South Carolina. When I was a kid, I remember hearing about South of the Border from a friend of mine that I grew up with in Richmond, Virginia who lived across the street from me. He and his family would go there a lot and he would talk about it. I am not sure I remember ever going there myself, although I remember going by there several times during family trips and seeing the prominent sombrero tower. [177]

After passing South of the Border, there was more construction that I cannot seem to get away from as well as cloudy skies and a little bit of a shower near Turbeville, South Carolina. It was nothing much and did not really shut me down at that point as I moved closer to the end point of where I was going – Summerton, South Carolina. That was where I had left off from my US 301 end-to-end ride in previous motorcycle trips. Goal met, now all that is left to complete US 301 is the last southern part down in Florida. Another day, perhaps.

After making it to Summerton, South Carolina, I started to try to make my way home and avoid the rain, so I rode on all kinds of back roads and made it up to SC Route 6 near Columbia, South Carolina. I managed to get to Interstate 20 West of Columbia and of course, they have been working on this stretch of I-20 for what seems like years and this day was no exception. I thought since I was just a little damp, I could dry out on the interstate by the time I rolled into Georgia. When I reached the Georgia State Line, I was almost totally dry and then there was a little shower just before getting home that got me a little bit damp again, but I made it home without getting very wet at all.

I got a picture of all the gear that I splayed out on the floor after getting home and getting everything unpacked from the saddle bags and then I was able to cover the bike.

My wife, Roxanna, and I went to the Texas Roadhouse for a reunion dinner and while we were in there awaiting our food to be delivered, the bottom fell out and it rained like crazy. I was glad I got home a little bit earlier than I thought would, so I beat all that rain. So, I did pretty well all in all. As a matter of fact, for the whole trip I did not experience any really bad weather where I had to spend a whole day through hard rain or anything of that sort.

Praise God I was able to just have a great peaceful trip in an awesome country with the freedom to actually ride through and see it. Awesome, indeed.

The Highway Diner is right next to Black Cat Harley-Davidson® and the Candlewood Suites

The U-turn Breakfast

Rocky
Mount,
North
Carolina

Corn
on one
side
tobacco
on the
other

Will I
be wet
or dry?

A short
shower
just to
be a
nuisance

Remember
South of
the Border
as a kid ?

Made it
home
and
unloaded
the bike
before
the
bottom
fell out

PHOTO MONTAGES

Bikers Along the Way

Boxes Along the Way

Construction Along the Way

Roundabouts Along the Way

Quotes and References

[1] https://www.harley-davidson.com/us/en/owners/hog/ride-365.html

[1a] "Similar to many other coastal counties, Beaufort County (then known as Pamptecough Precinct) was formed out of the larger Bath County in 1705. By 1712, the county received its formal name, which is attributed to Henry Somerset, Duke of Beaufort, and one of North Carolina's Lords Proprietors.

Although Beaufort was formally recognized in the early-eighteenth century, the area's history predates the county's establishment. English explorers trekked across what is now Beaufort County, encountering the Tuscarora Indians and establishing permanent settlements by the 1690s. One such settlement grew into Bath, the state's first incorporated town. Over time, the settlements became towns, burgeoning largely because of access to navigable waters."

https://co.beaufort.nc.us/tourism/history-of-beaufort-county

[2] "The Blue Star Memorial Highways are a tribute to the armed forces that have defended the United States of America. The National Garden Clubs, Inc., is the parent organization for Blue Star Memorial Highways.

The idea dates to 1944 when the New Jersey State Council of Garden Clubs beautified a 5½-mile stretch of U.S. 22 from Mountainside to North Plainfield. Approximately 8,000 dogwood trees were planted as a living memorial to the men and women in the Armed Forces from New Jersey. The Blue Star, taken from the blue star in the service flag, was chosen to symbolize the memorial because it was used during World War II on flags and homes of families that had a son or daughter in the service."

https://www.fhwa.dot.gov/infrastructure/blue01.cfm

[3] "Isle of Wight County is one of the oldest county governments in the United States of America. Nestled on the shores of Virginia's James River, Isle of Wight's residents enjoy the rural nature of the county coupled with the quaint atmosphere of the two incorporated towns, Smithfield and Windsor."

https://www.co.isle-of-wight.va.us/

[4] While the quote here is for the photo on the referenced site, it still fits my photo as well.

"The US-17 James River Bridge, looking northeast toward Newport News. The shipping channel is crossed by a 415-foot-long vertical lift span that has 60 feet of vertical clearance when closed. There are no naval installations upstream of this bridge, although there are civilian port facilities in Hopewell and Richmond. The James River Bridge is 4.5 miles long. Starting just off the right edge of the photo is Northrop Grumman Newport News (formerly named Newport News Shipbuilding and Drydock Company)."

http://www.roadstothefuture.com/US17_JRB.html

[5] Another interesting site depicting the James River Bridge has the following information:

"The 4.5-mile James River Bridge, Virginia's longest state-maintained bridge, opened in 1928 as the first connector between the Peninsula and South Hampton Roads. The bridge carries Routes 17/258/32 between Newport News and Isle of Wight County. The original two-lane bridge was replaced in 1982 with a wider four-lane lift span bridge designed to handle increased traffic volumes. With nearly one million vehicles using the JRB each month, this crossing offers a smart travel alternative when the Hampton Roads Bridge-Tunnel and Monitor-Merrimac Bridge-Tunnel are congested."

http://www.virginiadot.org/travel/hro-tunnel-default.asp#The_Bridges

[6] "Legend has it that Cornwallis' Cave (hidden across from the bustling beach) is where the British General retreated to avoid bombardment during the Battle of Yorktown. The National Park Service has long since claimed research shows otherwise.

In reality, the cave dates back to before the Revolution, and was likely used for potato storage during colonial times…."

https://www.virginia.org/Listings/HistoricSites/CornwallisCave/

[7] Rick Lambert did a great job researching and documenting the facts and stories in his work, "Cornwallis Cave, Lord Cornwallis Cave".

"Cornwallis Cave is a small cave with a history larger than the cave itself. Being almost entirely manmade, it was reputed to be the hiding place of the British General Charles Cornwallis during the Yorktown siege. It was a commercial operation by 1848 and into the early 1900s. Now owned by the National Park Service, visitors are prevented from entering the cave and it is no longer believed to be the hiding place of General Cornwallis."

http://virginiacaves.org/images/other/CornwallisCave/CornwallisCave.pdf

[8] "When British General Lord Charles Cornwallis and his army surrendered to General George Washington's American force and its French allies at the Battle of Yorktown on October 19, 1781, it was more than just military win. The outcome in Yorktown, Virginia marked the conclusion of the last major battle of the American Revolution and the start of a new nation's independence. It also cemented Washington's reputation as a great leader and eventual election as first president of the United States."

https://www.history.com/topics/american-revolution/siege-of-yorktown

[9] "The George P. Coleman Bridge is a double-swing span that connects Gloucester Point and Yorktown. The bridge was constructed in 1952 as a two-lane bridge, designed to carry up to 15,000 vehicles a day. In 1995, the bridge was reconstructed with four lanes to handle increased traffic. Almost a million vehicles cross each month."

http://www.virginiadot.org/travel/hro-tunnel-default.asp#The_Bridges

[10] "Port Royal is famous because it was once a nexus for international shipping, playing host to a bustling port that unloaded goods that were shipped from other countries. Ships would sail up the Chesapeake Bay, up the Rappahannock River, and stop at Port Royal. Goods would be unloaded here and then were taken by ground to other parts of the country. The ships brought wealth to Port Royal, and with wealth came the construction of the homes on the walking tour."

http://www.historicportroyal.net/places-to-visit/

[11] The Northern Neck website captures the essence of some of the history of Virginia:

"This peninsula nestled between the Potomac and the Rappahannock Rivers and spilling into the Chesapeake Bay was part of the enormous 1649 land grant by Charles II, known as the Fairfax Grant. The bountiful waters of the Potomac and Rappahannock Rivers, and the Chesapeake Bay supported and induced English settlement. The English built stately homes and farmed tobacco for export to England, which became the basis of the Northern Neck's economy during the Colonial era. The Northern Neck's most famous son, George Washington, born on Pope's Creek off the Potomac River, called the region "the Garden of Virginia." Our nation's fifth president, James Monroe, was born in Westmoreland County in 1758.

The Lee family of Virginia called the Northern Neck home and built Stratford Hall in the 1730s of bricks fired from the clay soil on the premises. A son of Thomas Lee, Richard Henry Lee, co-wrote the Westmoreland Resolves, which proposed American independence in 1766 in protest against the Stamp Act. Richard Henry Lee and his brother Francis Lightfoot Lee were the only two brothers to sign the Declaration of Independence. The last Lee to survive to maturity, Robert E. Lee, was born at Stratford Hall in 1807."

https://www.northernneck.org/the-northern-neck-2/

[12] "Easton….is situated in the tidewater region along the eastern shore of Chesapeake Bay, near the head of Tred Avon River (estuary). It was settled by Quakers in 1682 and established as a town in 1710 when the area was chosen as the site of the county courthouse (built c. 1712). The town was called Talbot Court House until 1789, when the present name, probably attributable to Easton, England, was adopted."

https://www.britannica.com/place/Easton-Maryland

[13] "The Pearl Harbor Memorial Bridge, on Route 50, also known as the Severn River Bridge, connects Annapolis to roads leading east. The bridge was officially named and dedicated in 2006, on the 65th anniversary of the attack on Pearl Harbor."

https://annapolisdiscovered.com/over-the-bridges/

[14] https://www.virginia.org/cities/Aldie/

[15] "Middleburg is located in Loudon County in the Northern Virginia Region of Virginia. Since the early 20th century, Middleburg gained a reputation as the "Nation's Horse and Hunt Capital," drawing in distinguished and well-known visitors from all over the U.S.

The National Sporting Library is Middleburg's state-of-the-art research facility dedicated to the world of horse sports, shooting and fishing, featuring an extensive, unique collection of over 16,000 books. Some manuscripts found in this library date as far back as the 17th century!"

https://www.virginia.org/cities/middleburg

[16] "The historic village of Upperville in Virginia's horse country is well-known in equestrian circles. However, located just 50 miles from downtown Washington, D.C., this exclusive enclave is an ideal escape for those "Inside the Beltway" too.

Founded in the late 18th Century, Upperville is an unincorporated village in Fauquier County, bordered by Loudoun, Clarke and Prince William counties. Upperville is a small hamlet that's often coupled with nearby Middleburg."

https://www.mansionglobal.com/articles/upperville-virginia-horse-country-with-an-upscale-twist-43706

[17] https://winchesterhistory.org/

[18] https://oldtownwinchesterva.com/

[19] https://wvtourism.com/town-guide-romney/

[20] "Clarksburg was named in 1778 for General George Rogers Clark and incorporated in 1785.

During the Civil War, it served as a supply depot of the Union Army from 1861 to 1865. General George B. McClellan had his headquarters here in 1861 until the Battle of Bull Run.

Clarksburg is the birthplace of General Thomas J. 'Stonewall' Jackson."

https://www.cityofclarksburgwv.com/270/Proud-Past

[21] Parkersburg is also home to the birth of the nation's oil and gas industry and the world's oldest producing oil well.

Today, one of the main attractions Parkersburg is known for is Blennerhassett Island where plans were developed by Aaron Burr and Harman Blennerhassett to undertake a military expedition to the Southwest.

http://parkersburgcity.com/pc/about/history/

[22] "Members of the Ohio Company of Associates sent the first settlers into the area in 1797. At first, the newcomers cleared and farmed their land and made no attempt to build a town. After more settlers arrived in 1798, local residents established Athens."

"According to the federal government's requirements, the Ohio Company of Associates had to establish an institution of higher education within its land grant. The company leaders chose Athens as the site for the school that eventually became known as Ohio University."

https://ohiohistorycentral.org/w/Athens,_Ohio

[23] https://www.stewmac.com/

[24] "Seip Mound is one of the largest earthen mounds built by the Hopewell culture (100 B.C. - 500 A.D.) of prehistoric Native American people. It is 240 feet long, 130 feet wide, and 30 feet high. Originally, this mound was surrounded by a large, semi-circular enclosure that was connected to smaller circular and square enclosures. In all, the earthworks enclosed 121 acres with 10,000 feet of embankment walls. The walls were up to ten feet in height."

https://ohiohistorycentral.org/w/Seip_Mound_and_Earthworks

[25] Medora Covered Bridge, Medora, Indiana is "the longest covered bridge in the USA whose historic framework is just as it was when built in 1875 with some repairs, but no structural changes because it did not have to be upgraded to meet modern vehicle standards."

http://www.medoracoveredbridge.com/

[26] George Rogers Clark National Historical Park, Vincennes, Indiana:

"The British flag would not be raised above Fort Sackville Feb. 25, 1779. At 10 a.m., the garrison surrendered to American Colonel George Rogers Clark. His American army, aided by French residents of the Illinois country, had marched through freezing floodwaters to gain this victory. The fort's capture assured United States claims to the frontier, an area nearly as large as the original 13 states."

https://www.nps.gov/gero/index.htm

Crossing the Wabash River into Illinois on the Lincoln Memorial Bridge to get back to US 50 West.

"The bridge, when it was built, would carry US 50 across the Wabash from Vincennes, Indiana, to Lawrence County, Illinois. It would become a major link in that road for several decades. It would be a replacement of a bridge that spanned the Wabash from Main Street in Vincennes for many years."

"The Abraham Lincoln Memorial Bridge still stands today, almost 90 years after the concrete structure was built. Yes, US 50 has been rerouted around Vincennes. The bridge now serves as Indiana State Road 441."

https://intransporthistory.home.blog/2020/08/17/vincennes-the-lincoln-memorial-bridge/

[27] https://www.historic66.com/

[28] "It is with good reason that Sedalia, Missouri has become central to the Joplin story and the site of the annual Scott Joplin Ragtime Festival. While Sedalia was Scott Joplin's home for only a few years, it was a home with a special meaning for him."

"Following the marriage [to Freddie Alexander in June 1904], the couple traveled by train to Sedalia stopping at towns along the way so that Joplin could give concerts. Early in July they arrived in Sedalia where Joplin continued to perform. Tragically, Freddie developed a cold that progressed into pneumonia, and died at the age of 20 on September 10, 1904, ten weeks after their marriage.

After Freddie's funeral, Joplin left Sedalia and never returned.

https://www.scottjoplin.org

[29] "In 2015, a new collaborative initiative was begun to bring together the Liberty Center Association for the Arts, the Scott Joplin International Ragtime Festival and the Sedalia Heritage Foundation and its Ragtime Archive Project. In 2016, Sedalia's Central Business and Cultural District became involved by erecting a plaque at 114 East Fifth Street, the former address of John Stark's business where he and Joplin executed the Maple Leaf Rag publishing contract."

https://www.scottjoplin.org

[30] "The Missouri-Kansas-Texas Railroad, better known as The Katy, was a large granger that maintained an unconventional north-south network within a region dominated by the Santa Fe, Missouri Pacific, and Southern Pacific/

St. Louis Southwestern (Cotton Belt). It was also forced to compete against the Rock Island and St. Louis-San Francisco (Frisco). In spite of this, the company suffered only one true bankruptcy as a result of financial hardship. As its name implies, the MKT linked its namesake states with key connections to St. Louis, Kansas City, Dallas/Fort Worth, Waco, San Antonio, and Galveston/Houston. Much of its growth across Texas occurred during the Jay Gould era, one of the industry's most notorious tycoons."

https://www.american-rails.com/mkt.html

[31] The history of this Katy Line station goes something like this:

"The M-K-T Builds a Landmark

The decision to build the new Katy Depot not only led Sedalia officials and townspeople to envision yet another chapter in the city's enduring relationship with the railroad, it also provided the railroad with the opportunity to advance its agenda in setting the pace for a new generation of depot building. In a broader sense, the move signified the importance of Sedalia in the history and development of the Missouri, Kansas and Texas Railroad as well as the railroad's importance to the history and development of Sedalia."

"After being abandoned by the Missouri-Kansas-Texas Railroad in 1983, the Missouri Department of Natural Resources received title to the depot as part of the 200 mile Katy Trail State Park. Wulff Rodgers Construction, Columbia, Missouri, received the state's contract for both the exterior and interior renovation. Funding for the renovation was provided by federal and state funds with local participation. S.B.W.E., Sedalia were the architects."

https://www.katydepotsedalia.com/

[32] Entering Emporia, Kansas where bicycles "have had a colorful past since their ancient beginnings in the 15th century up to today."

"Described as "the loveliest site in the world for a town," Emporia was founded by five men from Lawrence in 1857, when Kansas was still a territory battling over slavery. The town charter prohibited gambling and the sale of liquor, making Emporia the first prohibition town in the world – 61 years before National Prohibition. Touting a squeaky clean image and free-state values, Emporia sprang up quickly. By the 1880s, Emporia had established two colleges and had become known as "the Athens of the Plains." Several of our downtown buildings date to this time period."

https://visitemporia.com/?s=history

[33] Some interesting facts and history:

The Atchison, Topeka & Santa Fe railroad was completed and the first passenger train entered Newton on July 17, 1871;

http://www.kancoll.org/books/cutler/harvey/harvey-co-p1.html

[34] "On August 20, 1871, one of the largest gunfights to ever take place in the American West was fought in Newton, Kansas. Known as the Hyde Park Gunfight or the Newton Massacre, the shootout claimed more lives than many more famous gunfights such as Dalton Gang Gunfight at Coffeeville, Kansas or the Gunfight at the O.K. Corral in Tombstone, Arizona.

When the Santa Fe Railroad extended its line to Newton, Kansas in 1871, this new frontier town succeeded Abilene as the terminus of the Chisholm Trail. Like other Kansas cowtowns, Newton quickly filled up with saloons, gambling parlors, brothels, and inevitably — lawless and violent men.

The whole affair began when two local lawmen by the names of Billy Bailey and Mike McCluskie argued over local politics on August 11th in the Red Front Saloon."

https://www.legendsofamerica.com/hyde-park-gunfight/

[35] "As the railroad expanded in Kansas, the trail changed a number of times and by the early 1870s, the cattle business in Abilene had diminished. In its place, new cattle markets at Ellsworth and Newton were established. The Chisholm Trail moved south to Newton in 1871 and the city became one of the most notorious and violent cattle

towns that ever existed. Just a year later, Wichita acquired the railroad and, along with it, the cattle business, which it retained until 1876. By 1880, the cattle only had to be driven to Caldwell, which competed with another popular cow town – Dodge City."

https://www.legendsofamerica.com/we-chisholmtrail/

[36] "The Railroad Savings & Loan Building [at the corner on the left] was built in 1925 in the Beaux Arts architectural style and designed by Greenebaum, Hardy and Schumacher. The Railroad Savings & Loan Company was chartered in May 1896 and it became one of the more prominent financial institutions in Newton, and Kansas, during the early 20th century. At the time when the new building was commissioned, the company was valued at $8 million."

https://www.newtonkansas.com/

[37] "The course plays on the town's railroad history, and many holes are, as they say in Scotland, "hard by the cinders," continuing a century's old tradition of golf bordering railways. We have also recreated the famous Road Hole green on our 16th Hole, which once sat adjacent to a railway. Another replicates the famous "Redan" from North Berwick, Scotland. Other holes have characteristics of early American holes, which also fronted railways at one time. The 12th hole for example, is similar to the fourth at the National Golf Links of America, one of our early classics. The ninth features a small platform green; typical of early American courses while the green on the par 5 fourth has some wild contours, seldom built these days."

https://www.sandcreekgolfclub.com/course-details/

[38] "While the Warkentins today are remembered primarily for the historical significance (and National Register status) of their Halstead farm and Newton home and mill (also a national landmark like the farm), during their lifetimes they achieved recognition for their entrepreneurship and support of their community.

Warkentin created what could be considered a business empire, owning another flour mill in Blackwell, Oklahoma, and serving as a director/owner of the Bank of Halstead, Kansas State Bank of Newton, Millers' National Insurance Company, the Terminal Warehouse Company, and the Western States Portland Cement Company. He was one of Newton's leading businessmen.

However, Bernhard Warkentin's leadership is perhaps best recognized today for his role in making Kansas into the "wheat" state. Growing wheat did not dominate Kansas agriculture in the early 1870s. Warkentin helped to shift farmers from planting spring and soft wheat to hard winter wheat. Warkentin encouraged farmers to grow Turkey Red Wheat from Russia, which was more suited to the Kansas climate and which his new steel roller mills could refine into excellent flour. In 1900 he worked with several groups to import 15,000 bushels of Turkey Red seed from Russia. Some debate surrounds the story of how Kansas became America's breadbasket, but the innovation and promotion of Bernhard Warkentin played a major role. Moreover, Kansas Mennonites soon became well known for their wheat production."

https://www.warkentinhouse.org/

[39] https://www.hmdb.org/m.asp?m=56848

[40] "In 1871 H.L. Sitler constructed a sod house 5 miles west of Fort Dodge on the Santa Fe Trail. Within one year this site grew into a town with a general store, 3 dance halls, and 6 saloons. Many of the early settlers of Dodge City were gamblers, gunslingers, and cattlemen. The Santa Fe Railroad reached Dodge City in 1872. Texas cattle drovers began to use a shortcut from the Chisholm Trail to Dodge City called the Texas Trail. Thousands of longhorn cattle were driven over the Texas Trail into Dodge City for loading on the railroad. With these cattle came cowboys, gamblers, buffalo hunters, and soldiers. Dodge City became a rowdy town famous for its saloons, outlaws, and Boot Hill Cemetery. Bat Masterson, and Wyatt Earp earned their fame as lawmen during this time."

https://www.dodgecity.org/420/Department-History

[41] The story of Boot Hill Beginnings can be found here:

"The first recorded killing in Dodge City was in September 1872, when an African-American man named Black Jack was shot for no reason by a gambler known as Denver. Shortly after that, Jack Reynolds was killed by a railroad track layer. In that first year, approximately fifteen men were killed in Dodge City, all being buried up on historical Boot Hill. Eventually, Boot Hill were have some 30 graves, including one female, Alice Chambers."

http://www.kansashistory.us/fordco/lawmen.html

[42] "A combination of unique geography and an elevation of 5,300 feet above sea level protect the city from harsh weather conditions, making Cañon City "the Climate Capital of Colorado," with temperatures generally 10 degrees warmer in Winter than other nearby Colorado communities."

"The first dinosaur bone discovered in Colorado was near Cañon City in late 1869 or early 1870. Over the next decade, scientists discovered many more dinosaur bones. In the 1880s Yale paleontologist Othniel C. Marsh, with the help of Cañon City resident Marshall P. Felch, discovered and named the Stegosaurus stenops, known commonly today as simply Stegosaurus."

"Fremont County comprises 1,533 square miles with an estimated population of 46,502. The county seat and largest city is Cañon City, located at the eastern mouth of the Royal Gorge of the Arkansas River."

"Tasked with conducting geographical survey of parts of the rural West, John C. Frémont first traveled through the Fremont County region in 1843, when he traveled up the Arkansas River to what is now Leadville. Between 1843 and 1852, Frémont conducted five expeditions that led him through land that would become Fremont County. He was supported by his guide, Kit Carson, whom Frémont popularized through accounts of their adventures. Frémont's reports portrayed Carson as a rugged mountain man, and his reputation grew throughout the country. Following his decade of expeditions, Frémont went on to serve as a politician and presidential candidate in the 1856 election."

https://coloradoencyclopedia.org/article/fremont-county

[43] "Two Benedictine monks came from Pennsylvania to Colorado to establish the Order of St. Benedict Monastery in 1886. Upon the building's completion, the monks opened a boarding school and made their first attempts at establishing a winery.

The school hit its height of popularity in the 1960s, after which enrollment steadily declined until the school was forced to close in 1985.

In order to find a new means of financial income, the Abbey's remaining 20 monks returned to the idea of establishing a vineyard. In 2000, they entrusted the production to a professional viticulturist who began producing wine the following year.

The winery and tasting room opened to the public in 2002, welcoming visitors to its beautiful and serene Rocky Mountain vineyard."

https://abbeywinery.com/about/

[44] "In the 1970s, Cañon City and other parts of Fremont County became popular destinations for film productions, particularly westerns. The Cowboys, starring John Wayne; The Duchess and the Dirtwater Fox, starring Goldie Hawn and George Segal; and How the West Was Won, starring James Arness and Bruce Boxleitner, were filmed in the surrounding area."

https://coloradoencyclopedia.org/article/fremont-county

[45] "Once called the Grand Canyon of the Arkansas River, the Royal Gorge is the county's most notable natural feature, drawing tribal and European inhabitants for centuries. Scientists concur that the gorge is the result of erosion alone. The Royal Gorge is approximately ten miles long with granite walls 1,000 feet high. The Arkansas River, one of the longest in the country, runs through the gorge.

In 1877, when silver was discovered in what would become Leadville, the D&RG in Cañon City and the Atchison, Topeka & Santa Fe Railway in Pueblo began an aggressive competition to extend a rail line to Leadville through the narrow Royal Gorge, which had space for only one rail line. In 1879, after gunfights between the two railroad crews and a legal battle that ended at the US Supreme Court, the D&RG was granted the primary right to build a line through the gorge. The D&RG line through the gorge allowed for increased transportation between cities in Fremont County and the mining camps in the mountains."

https://coloradoencyclopedia.org/article/fremont-county

[46] "The upper portion of the Arkansas River cascades out of the rugged Rocky Mountains and drops 10,000 feet in only 125 miles. This steep mountain torrent has several popular whitewater rafting sites and is noted for its exceptional trout fishing.

The middle portion extends across the Great Plains. After the Arkansas River rushes through the Royal Gorge at Cañon City, Colorado, it widens and flattens dramatically. Its gradient continues to decline as it moves onto the Great Plains west of Pueblo, Colorado, where it becomes a typical Great Plains river with a wide and shallow channel and a meandering flood plain that is subject to significant fluctuations in flow. Major tributaries include the Canadian and Cimarron rivers, each exceeding 600 miles in length.

The Arkansas River has played an important role in western expansion. Early explorers such as Zebulon Pike followed it westward. The river served as the boundary between the United States and Mexico from 1820 to 1846, and the Santa Fe Trail followed the Arkansas River through much of Kansas."

https://encyclopediaofarkansas.net/

[47] "The Colorado mountain town of Salida sits in the middle of the state, literally in the "Heart of the Rockies," about 2 hours from Colorado Springs and 3 hours from Denver.

Located in central Colorado in the Upper Arkansas River Valley, Salida has more than a dozen 14,000-foot tall mountain peaks, surpassing all other Colorado regions."

"Chaffee County was established in 1879 and named for Jerome Chaffee, Colorado's first United States Senator and local investor. The history of Chaffee County and the surrounding area is a rich mix of many influences, particularly cultural and economic forces. The area was originally settled by the Ute Indians, for whom many of the local mountain peaks are named. Early in its history, the area experienced an influx of explorers, miners, railroad expansionists, farmers, and ranchers. The influence of each has dwindled over the years, but their mark in the history of the Salida and central Colorado area is evident throughout the valley."

http://salida.com/

[48] "There are relatively few canyons on the west side of the San Rafael Swell, where the land slopes more gently and does not form the dramatic reef that characterizes the eastern edge. One of the best is Devils Canyon, a long drainage that starts just beneath the highest point in the Swell, 7,921 foot San Rafael Knob, and has eroded deep into generally dull-colored straticulate layers of Cedar Mesa sandstone that cover this region, forming some narrow sections and joined by many slot-like tributaries. All the canyon is close to Interstate 70 and is easily accessed yet is quite undisturbed and not often visited. At least two days is needed to fully explore this area though the best of the main gorge and several of the side branches can be visited on a day trip."

https://www.americansouthwest.net/slot_canyons/devils_canyon/index.html

[49] Preserving America's World War II POW Camps

By: Teresa Bergen

In Issue: May/June 2018

http://www.saturdayeveningpost.com/2018/04/19/in-the-magazine/preserving-americas-world-war-ii-pow-camps.html

Tami Olsen had never noticed two dilapidated buildings in her small town of Salina, Utah, until the mayor asked her father to restore them. "Dad was like, 'Okay, awesome, we have a project,'" Tami recalls. "And he just said 'we.'"

Suddenly Tami and Dee Olsen, an octogenarian retired engineer, were deep into a two-year project restoring a World War II prisoner of war camp that once housed 250 German prisoners. Now Camp Salina is open as a museum reviving this mostly forgotten piece of American history. Local families donated artifacts from the camp's POW days, including artwork and letters from prisoners who kept in touch long after armistice. One of the museum's prized possessions is a jewelry box a prisoner made from matchsticks and Popsicle sticks.

https://www.salinacity.org/ccc-pow-camp-salina-utah-featured-in-saturday-evening-post-preserving-americas-world-war-ii-pow-camps/

[50] Round Hill to Noon Rock Peak

"Noon Rock Peak is one of the Summits in Millard County, UT and can be found on the Scipio South USGS topographic quad map. The GPS coordinates are 39.1916271 (latitude), -112.1210461 (longitude) and the approximate elevation is 7,680 feet (2,341 meters) above sea level."

https://www.mountainzone.com/mountains/utah/millard-ut/summits/noon-rock-peak/

[51] "Vermont resident J. W. Long came to White Pine County in 1878 and soon set up a camp known as "Ely," after discovering gold. Ely was founded as a stagecoach station along the Pony Express and Central Overland Route. Ely's mining boom came later than the other towns along US 50, with the discovery of copper in 1906. This made Ely a mining town, suffering through the boom-and-bust cycles so common in the West."

http://elynevada.net/history/

[52] "The Nevada Northern Railway Complex is the best-preserved, least altered, and most complete main yard complex remaining from the steam railroad era. It was established in 1905 to support the area's booming copper mining industry. The era of dieselization of the railroad industry during the second half of the 20th century led to alterations and demolitions of railroad yards and shops nationwide. The East Ely yard escaped modernization because of its geographical remoteness and the decline of the mining industry it once served."

https://elynevada.net/nevada-northern-railway/

[53] "Nevada's rail history dates back to 1868 when the Central Pacific Railroad reached the state building east from Sacramento, California. The CP, of course, was a product of the Pacific Railroad Act of 1862, signed into law by President Abraham Lincoln, which sought to construct a Transcontinental Railroad. The CP would be the western railroad building east while the Union Pacific headed west from Omaha, Nebraska. As many know, of course, the two railroads met at Promontory Point, Utah completing the line on May 10, 1869. The CP would soon after become part of the Southern Pacific system. In the proceeding years the Silver State would be home to a number of celebrated western railroads."

https://www.american-rails.com/nv.html

[54] "In 1912, there were almost no good roads to speak of in the United States. The relatively few miles of improved road were only around towns and cities. A road was "improved" if it was graded; one was lucky to have gravel or brick. Asphalt and concrete were yet to come. Most of the 2½ million miles of roads were just dirt: bumpy and dusty in dry weather, impassable in wet weather. Worse yet, the roads did not really lead anywhere. They spread out aimlessly from the center of the settlement. To get from one settlement to another, it was much easier to take the train.

Carl Fisher recognized this situation, and an idea started to take hold. Fisher was a man of ideas. As soon as he thought of a project and got it started, he would grow restless and start on another one. His Indianapolis Motor Speedway was a success, especially after he paved it with brick and started the Indianapolis 500, and he would later turn a swamp into one of the greatest beach resorts: Miami Beach, Florida. However, in 1912, he dreamed of another grand idea: a highway spanning the continent, from coast to coast.

He called his idea the Coast-to-Coast Rock Highway. The gravelled road would cost about ten million dollars, low even for 1912. Communities along the route would provide the equipment and in return would receive free materials and a place along America's first transcontinental highway. The highway would be finished in time for the 1915 Panama-Pacific Exposition and would run from the exposition's host, San Francisco, to New York City."

https://www.lincolnhighwayassoc.org/history/

[55] "The news traveled as far away as South Dakota. The Deadwood Daily Pioneer-Times reported:

Eureka, Nev. July 23, [1909]. – The first gold bar ever produced in the Eureka district, being the product of the ore of the Windfall mine, was brought to Eureka recently from the Eureka Windfall Mining Company's new cyanide mine…It is a beautiful yellow bar, weighing a little over 700 ounces and valued at $12,000 to $14,000."

https://elkodaily.com/mining/eureka-s-windfall-birth-of-a-modern-gold-district-with-community-spirit/article_5bc8a16b-98c3-5d37-9766-4fa6ff99b3ff.html

[56] http://www.co.eureka.nv.us/Hwy%2050%20Visitor%20Guide%202011%20small.pdf

[57] "The Hickison Summit area of the Great Basin is rich in prehistoric and historic resources. Not only are there petroglyphs such as found here at the Hickison Petroglyph site, but there are numerous prehistoric hunting and living sites dating back as far as 10,000 BC. Historic sites include the trails of frontier explorers, John C. Fremont and James H. Simpson, the Pony Express Route, the Overland Stage Route, mining camps, and ranches."

https://www.roadtripryan.com/go/t/nevada/northern-nevada/hickison-petroglyph

[58] Hickison Summit is located on Highway 50, around 30 miles southeast of Austin at the northern end of the Toiyabe Range and situated within a pinyon forest. The site is located on the road to the ranch of John Hickerson (also an alternative spelling of the site name) after whom the site was named. This site was interpreted as a hunting locality by Trudy Thomas because the most common motif at the site was thought to represent "hoof prints."

http://www.onlinenevada.org/articles/hickison-summit

[59] "Named for Austin, Texas, Austin was founded in 1862, as part of a silver rush reputedly triggered by a Pony Express horse who kicked over a rock."

https://austinnevada.com/rich-history

[60] "The Austin Cemetery is located about a mile northwest of the built-up part of town on the north side of the lower end of Pony Canyon at an elevation of just over 6,200 feet above sea level. US Highway 50 runs through the cemetery east to west and the junction of US 50 and Nevada Highway 305 is located a short distance to the east. The cemetery is actually comprised of five cemeteries, (listed east to west): the Masonic and Odd Fellows sections on the north side of US 50 and the Calvary (Catholic) and Citizens cemeteries on the south side of US 50. A fifth cemetery, the Indian cemetery, is located west of the Citizen's section."

https://austinnevada.com/cemetery/

[61] "At the turn of the century Fallon was a "dusty crossroads" between St. Clair and Stillwater. The local Native Americans referred to it as "Jim's Town." Jim Richards operated his store very near Mike and Eliza Fallon's ranch house and post office, which had been established in 1896.

Soon rumors flew about a project to build a dam and canal to irrigate, or "reclaim", desert lands. Following the assassination of President McKinley in 1901, longtime conservationist Theodore Roosevelt became President. He soon signed the papers which established the Reclamation Act of 1902 and a federal reclamation system began financed from the sale of public lands. The Reclamation Act also created the United States Reclamation Service (USRS)."

https://www.fallonchamber.com/

[62] "President Abraham Lincoln, recognizing the importance of Nevada's silver and gold to the Union's Civil War effort, signed the proclamation that ushered Nevada into statehood on October 31, 1864. Carson City was selected as the state capital at the constitutional convention…"

"Following the discovery of gold and silver on the nearby Comstock Lode in 1859, Carson City became a thriving commercial center. To their astonishment and delight of its citizens, the discovery of the Comstock Lode brought their Carson City to life as a freight and transportation center."

https://www.carson.org/residents/history

[63] "The famous Virginia and Truckee Railroad which was headquartered in Carson City went out of business in 1950. The Committee identified a piece of V&T property currently a part of railroad magnate, Darius Ogden Mill's Estate as having park potential. Upon receiving a favorable response from the Mills estate the Park Committee initiated negations to obtain the acreage which was located at the eastern edge of the city and known informally as "Foley's Forest". In 1951 the Estate sold to the City of Carson"…for and in consideration of the sum of ten dollars ($10.00), lawful money of the United States…" approximately 50 acres for the park with the stipulation that it be known as Mill's Park in honor of its benefactor, D.O. Mills."

https://www.nevadawomen.org/research-center/biographies-alphabetical/edith-naomi-bremenkampf-bernard/

[64] "The Carson & Mills Park Railroad is a two-foot (narrow gauge) railroad that the whole family will enjoy. Ride behind a replica of a diesel switcher engine and choose an open gondola or a covered passenger car. The 1-1/4 mile trip takes you through beautiful Mills Park and lasts approximately 15 minutes."

https://www.carson.org/government/departments-g-z/parks-recreation-open-space/parks-and-open-space/mills-park/carson-city-railroad-association

[65] "The Carson Range is a subsection of the greater Sierra Nevada range, which runs most of the length of California. At just 50 miles (80km) long and 5-10 miles (8-16km) wide, the Carson Range is not huge, but it is large enough to create a rain shadow that covers most of the greater Reno and Carson City areas.

Three-fourths of the Carson Range is within the state of Nevada, while the northern and southernmost sections are in California. The range is also the northernmost section of the Sierra Nevada that has true alpine territory, as the rest of the mountains north of the Carson Range are mostly at or under 8,000 ft (2,438m) in elevation."

https://peakvisor.com/range/carson-range.html

[66] https://visitinglaketahoe.com/facts/

[67] Redwood National Park - Kuechel Visitor Center near Orick, California.

"Traditional homes of the region's American Indians usually were constructed of planks split from fallen redwoods. These houses were built over pits dug beneath the building, with the space between the pit and the walls forming a natural bench. A house was understood to be a living being. The redwood that formed its planks was itself the body of one of the Spirit Beings. Spirit Beings were believed to be a divine race who existed before humans in the redwood region and who taught people the proper way to live here.

Once gold was discovered along northwestern California's Trinity River in 1850, outsiders moved into the area in overwhelming numbers. The initial contact with native peoples was gruesome.

The newcomers pushed the American Indians off their land, hunted them down, scorned, raped, and enslaved them. Resistance – and many of the American Indians did resist – was often met with massacres. Militia units composed of unemployed miners and homesteaders set forth to rid the countryside of "hostile" Indians, attacking villages and, in many documented cases, slaughtering men, women, and even infants. Upon their return, these killers were treated as heroes, and paid by the state government for their work.

Treaties that normally allotted American Indians reservations were never ratified in this part of California. Although treaties were signed, the California delegation lobbied against them on the grounds that they left too much land in Indian hands. Reservations were thus never established by treaty, but rather by administrative decree.

To this day, the displacement of many tribes, the lack of treaty guarantees, and the absence of federal recognition of their sovereignty continue to cloud the legal rights of many American Indians."

https://www.nps.gov/redw/learn/historyculture/area-history.htm

[68] "When Euro-Americans swept westward in the 1800s, they needed raw material for their homes and lives.

Commercial logging followed the expansion of America as companies struggled to keep up with the furious pace of progress. Timber harvesting quickly became the top manufacturing industry in the west.

When gold was discovered in northwestern California in 1850, the rush was on. Thousands crowded the remote redwood region in search of riches and new lives. These people were no less dependent upon lumber, and the redwoods conveniently provided the wood the people needed. The size of the huge trees made them prized timber, as redwood became known for its durability and workability. By 1853, nine sawmills were at work in Eureka, a gold boom town established three years prior due to the gold boom. Large-scale logging was soon underway, and the once immense stands of redwoods began to disappear by the close of the 19th century.

At first, axes, saws, and other early methods of bringing the trees down were used. But the loggers made use of rapidly improving technology in the 20th century that allowed more trees to be harvested in less time. Transportation also caught up to the task of moving the massive logs. The locomotive replaced horses and oxen. The era of railroad logging became the fastest way to transport the logs to mills."

https://www.nps.gov/redw/learn/historyculture/area-history.htm

[69] "In March 1964, Battery Point Lighthouse withstood a destructive tsunami that raged over Crescent City. Topping out at 21 feet, the largest wave slammed into 29 city blocks of the town, causing millions of dollars in damage. The disaster left a mark on Crescent City. To understand why Crescent City got the nickname "Comeback Town, USA" take the historic walking tour through downtown. You'll amble around memorials, high-water lines, murals and impactful images comparing architecture before and after.

Though the tsunami was a shattering event, it was a true marker of how resilient and generous the people of Crescent City can be. And history has a strange way of repeating itself. Almost 50 years after the disaster, a tiny boat from Japan washed up along the town's shore. Lost at sea after surviving a tsunami across the ocean in Japan, the Kamome boat became a symbol that would connect two resilient cities forever."

https://visitdelnortecounty.com/article/crescent-city-travel-guide/

[70] "During the early 1850s hundreds of miners and settlers poured into southwest Oregon and onto Indian lands staking claims and establishing farms. The clash of cultural attitudes toward the ownership and use of natural resources led to the Rogue River Indian Wars of 1853-56.

War came to the coast in March of 1856, when the "Tu-tu-tuni" attacked Ellensburg, a settlement at the mouth of the Rogue River (present-day Gold Beach). A party of 34 armed civilians, led by vigilante George H. Abbott, raced northward along the coast from Crescent City, California in advance of regular army troops dispatched to assist survivors who had assembled just north of Ellensburg at Fort Miner. Local "Chet-less-chun-dunn" villagers responded with armed resistance near this site holding the party at bay behind driftwood for several days until army troops arrived.

This conflict led to the tracking and killing of those Indians who participated in the battle. A few "Chet-less-chun-dunne" still reside in communities along the Oregon and northern California coast."

https://theoregoncoast.info/History/ConflictatPistolRiver.html

[71] "The City of Gold Beach sits just south of the Rogue River, about forty miles north of the California state line. The section of coastline received its name after placer miners discovered gold in the sands near the mouth of the Rogue River in 1852. The town, initially named Ellensburg, was incorporated in 1853. Ellensburg was the namesake of Sarah Ellen Tichenor, the daughter of sea captain William Tichenor, who established the coastal town of Port Orford, about thirty miles to the north. In 1858, Ellensburg was named county seat because Port Orford had failed to finance the construction of an adequate courthouse."

"On March 25, 1890, the Ellensburg postmaster changed the name of the post office to Gold Beach to avoid confusion with Ellensburg, Washington. "Although the post office at this place has been changed to Gold Beach," the July 10, 1890, Gold Beach Gazette reported, "the name of the county seat will continue to be Ellensburg until changed by an act of the legislature." The name of the town and, consequently, the county seat was officially changed to Gold Beach on January 23, 1891."

https://www.oregonencyclopedia.org/articles/gold_beach/#.X5ChgtBKheU

[72] "The Isaac Lee Patterson Bridge across the Rogue River on Highway 101 at Gold Beach is depicted above at the time of its completion in 1931; it was dedicated on May 28, 1932.

Through the end of the nineteenth century, the rugged Oregon coastline could be walked on a network of trails that paralleled the shore or followed the hard sand beaches, crossing the many coastal streams by ford, canoe, or ferry. There were few good ports on the coast, and regular ocean-going service did connect, for example, ports on Coos Bay and Yaquina Bay with San Francisco and Portland. But no service ever connected Coos Bay with other coastal points such as Tillamook or Reedsport. The establishment of a road the length of the coastline was not seriously pursued until the 1920s. Depression-era public works projects helped to push the completion of what was called the Roosevelt Highway in 1940."

https://www.oregonhistoryproject.org/articles/historical-records/rogue-river-bridge-gold-beach/#.X5Cf69BKheU

[73] "February 10, 1937 was a very windy day. The 75 miles per hour wind caused the steam schooner Cottoneva to run aground at Battle Rock. The 190 foot schooner was in port loading 800,000 board feet of lumber. The captain and all 26 seamen were rescued by the coast guard using a breecher buoy.

The Cottoneva was constructed in 1917, and was originally called Frank D. Stout. The only thing left of the schooner, is the propeller. The propeller.... is on display in the Battle Rock park located in Port Orford, Oregon."

https://theoregoncoast.info/Shipwrecks/Cottoneva.html

[74] "In 2001 over 32.1 million pounds of seafood, valued at nearly $18 million dollars was landed. Over the years these values will fluctuate due to environmental constraints and management policies. Most of the seafood products from the south coast are either sold fresh or frozen in the California, Midwest, and East Coast markets or are exported to Europe and Japan. Not only do the landings add dollars to the local economy, but also the majority of the processing of seafood is done along the southern coast. This, combined with the service industry in marine repair, fabrication and other services, expands the contribution of the seafood industry to the economic well-being of the area."

https://coosbaynorthbendcharlestonchamber.com/bay-area-info/business-info/major-industries/

[75] "Of all the bridges engineer Conde B. McCullough designed, the one on Highway 101 that spans Coos Bay was his favorite. This impressive bridge was renamed the Conde B. McCullough Memorial Bridge in 1947, the year after McCullough died. The bridge was part of the federally funded Coast Bridges Project, a Works Progress Administration (WPA) plan in 1934-1936 to build five bridges across coastal waterways in order to complete the Oregon Coast Highway. With its mix of Art Deco, Gothic, and Moderne design elements, the McCullough Memorial is one of the most recognizable icons of the Oregon coast.

Originally called the Coos Bay Bridge, at 5,305 feet it was the longest in the state highway system when it was completed in 1936. Because the 793-foot-wide navigation channel had to remain open during construction, McCullough designed a steel cantilevered truss mid-section, with the road deck reaching 150 feet above water. Temporary work bridges were built out to the piers where each cantilever section began. This provided access as well as a base to build temporary supports, as the arms of the cantilever sections extended over the work bridges. Although the construction resembled a giant erector set, the building of the 1,708-foot steel truss was considered an engineering triumph for its time. The steel truss is flanked on each side by several reinforced-concrete arches below the road deck, leading to entry plazas boasting elaborately embellished abutments and staircases."

https://www.oregonencyclopedia.org/articles/conde_b_mccullough_memorial_bridge/#.X5Df_NBKheU

[76] "The Umpqua River Lighthouse, Oregon's first, was built twice. The U.S. Office of Coast Survey in 1849 selected the mouth of the Umpqua River as one of the first sixteen lighthouse locations for the West Coast. The survey sought to identify locations for a string of lighthouses detectible to mariners in a line-of-sight, leaving no stretch of the coast beyond visual range. This presented challenges on the south coast along the fifty-five miles from Cape Arago to Heceta Head, which is mainly a dune field lacking rocky promontories. The chosen spot was Umpqua's low-lying, sandy north spit, roughly equidistant between those headlands."

https://www.oregonencyclopedia.org/articles/umpqua_river_lighthouse/#.X5FwvtBKheU

[77] "In many ways, the story of Reedsport is a microcosm of the story of Oregon. Since the mid-1800s, the town has seen economic booms driven by abundant natural resources and has endured long periods of bust as those resources dwindled and priorities changed. Reedsport has both flourished and floundered. The town is about two miles up the Umpqua River from Gardiner, south across the Reedsport Bridge near the mouth of the Umpqua River. Beginning in 1852, homesteaders resettled the area around what would become Reedsport, but the town was not platted and named until about 1900. The post office was established in 1912 and the town was incorporated in 1919."

https://www.oregonencyclopedia.org/articles/reedsport/#.X5FxXtBKheU

[78] "The first inhabitants of what we now know as the city of Florence were the Siuslaw people. In fact, these people began settling the coast approximately 9,000 years ago. The Siuslaw people have lived in the same locations for hundreds of generations. The Siuslaw and Lower Umpqua rivers and estuaries were the dominating factors in the local economy. Providing ample supplies of fish and shellfish, the rivers also served as a highway into the Coast Range.

Descendants of the Siuslaw people live today throughout Western Oregon, represented by federally recognized tribes. These include the Confederated Tribes of Coos, Lower Umpqua, and Siuslaw, and the Confederated Tribes of Siletz Indians.

If you are heading north on Highway 101, you will cross over into Florence via the historic Siuslaw River Bridge. With a quick right turn at the end of the bridge, you enter Florence's Historic Old Town District. The bridge is an Art Deco, double-leaf bascule bridge. Two movable sections rise upwards to open and allow the navigation of large ships and other water traffic to pass. The bridge is significant as one of five Depression-era bridges that completed the Oregon Coast Highway (Hwy 101) as part of the Coast Bridges Project. These five bridges, designed by civil engineer Conde McCullough, were built between 1934 and 1936 under the Public Works Administration (PWA). The bridge opened in March 1936 and added to the National Register of Historic Places on August 5, 2005."

https://riverhouseflorence.com/history-of-florence/

[79] The Oregon Coast Highway

"Many places on the Oregon coast were virtually inaccessible in the early twentieth century. Small fishing villages existed as remote outposts, separated by rocky headlands and timber-covered hills. The Roosevelt Coast Military Highway, named in honor of President Theodore Roosevelt, was a result of a renewed national sense of isolationism and the perceived need for emergency preparedness following World War I. In 1919, Oregon voters approved the sale of $2.5 million in bond obligations for the project, but matching federal funds failed to materialize.

By the early 1920s, however, a pleasure-seeking public asked for coastal highway construction. Work on the new coast road, designed by the state's highway department, began in earnest in 1921. Throughout the 1920s, crews graded and paved section after section of the 400-mile route. In 1926, the road became U.S. 101; in 1931, the state renamed it the Oregon Coast Highway."

https://www.oregonencyclopedia.org/articles/highway_101_oregon_coast_highway_/#.X5Fx5NBKheU

[80] Sea Lions Cave Area

"Eleven miles north of Florence on U.S. Highway 101 are the remains of an ice-age beach of seafloor basalt, where waves hit fracture zones in the hard basalt to carve what is now Sea Lion Caves, the world's largest sea cave. The main attraction is the sea lions, which sixteenth-century Spanish sailors referred to as lobos marinos, or sea wolves, perhaps because of their doglike yelps.

In 1880, Captain William Cox was the first non-Native to discover the cave, which consists of a 325-foot headland on two acres of stone "floors" and tumbled ledges upon which the present gift shop and entrance to the cave stands. In 1926, R.E. Clanton purchased the property from the Cox estate, and he was joined in his business enterprise by J.G. Houghton and J.E. Jacobson. In 1929, the original partners dropped a rope ladder to a primitive footbridge, leading to the north entrance to the cave. Sea Lion Caves opened formally to the public in 1932."

https://www.oregonencyclopedia.org/articles/sea_lion_caves/#.X5F1r9BKheU

[81] "Yachats (say YAH-hots) was named after the Yachats River, and is a word derived from native local languages. Ya'Xaik (YAH-hike) was the Alseas' word for the locale."

https://www.yachats.org/

[82] In 1847, Jeremiah Ralston came into the area with his "train of three wagons and was the first to map the town and name it. He chose the name because the many cedar trees by the river made him think of the Biblical references to the cedars of Lebanon and partly because of sentiment for his birth place – Lebanon, Tennessee."

https://www.ci.lebanon.or.us/community/page/history-lebanon-oregon

[83] For more information and insight, review the lebanon_history.pdf at:

https://www.ci.lebanon.or.us/sites/default/files/fileattachments/utility_services/page/726/lebanon_history.pdf

[84] "Located between the western slope of the Cascade Range and the folding hills of the Willamette Valley near Sweet Home, Foster Reservoir is one of the 13 reservoirs in the Willamette Valley that was built by the U.S. Corps of Army Engineers between 1961 and 1968. Foster Reservoir confines water from the middle and south forks of the Santiam River. Construction of Foster Dam was done consecutively with Green Peter Dam.

Both reservoirs and dams are operated together to serve for the purposes of hydroelectric power generation, water retention, flood damage prevention, and irrigation. Foster Dam is a rock-fill construction of 126 feet high and 4,565 feet wide, with a storage size of 61,000 acre-feet. When full, Foster Reservoir covers about 494 ha (1,220 acres) and Green Peter – 1,505 ha (3,720 acres). The length of Green Peter and Foster Lakes are 1,500 ft (457 m) and 4,565 ft (1,391 m) accordingly. The reservoirs provide habitat for rare species such as the northern spotted owl, western pond turtle, steelhead, cutthroat trout and Chinook salmon."

https://oregondiscovery.com/foster-reservoir

[85] https://www.waymarking.com/waymarks/wm4YHA_EB_Three_Sisters_Viewpoint

[86] "The historical growth of Vale begins with the Native American tribes living along the banks of the Malheur River, close to where Willow Creek enters from the north and Bully Creek enters from the west. Life in this area centers around the hot springs that flow into Malheur River from under Rinehart Butte. With the super heated water flowing into the river, caves on the butte to dwell in and lots of salmon running in season, this area was a central gathering place for the Paiute Indians. The salmon runs were a primary gathering time for the people, who mostly lived in small groups the rest of the year."

https://www.cityofvale.com/about/history/

[87] "Vale's Outdoor Art Gallery has 25 murals depicting Vale's history on the Oregon Trail on the walls of various buildings throughout the town and on four metal murals placed outside the city limits welcoming visitors. Founded in November of 1992 by individuals who were interested in revitalizing Vale's economy and possibly providing economic growth through tourism, the Mural Society paints new murals each year. The money for the murals is raised through donations, a live auction and a street sale. In addition, the mural society receives grants, but money from the community is still its primary source of funding."

https://traveloregon.com/things-to-do/culture-history/historic-sites-oregon-trail/vale-murals/

[88] "The Vidalia Onion Story takes root in Toombs County, Georgia over 80 years ago when a farmer by the name of Moses Coleman discovered in the late spring of 1931 the onions he had planted were not hot as he expected. They were sweet! It was a struggle to sell the onions at first, but Moses persevered, and managed to sell them for $3.50 per 50-pound bag, which in those days was a big price.

Other farmers, who through the Depression years had not been able to get a fair price for their produce, thought Coleman had found a gold mine. They began to follow suit, and soon after, their farms were also producing the sweet, mild onion."

https://www.vidaliaonions.com/history/

[89] "Nyssa was founded in 1883. When the Oregon Short Line Railroad came through southern Idaho and Eastern Oregon, the town sprang up. It was a watering station between Ontario, Oregon and Parma, Idaho for many years. Eventually it grew into a trading station also.

There are several versions of how the town was named. One is that it is an Indian word which means sagebrush. The second is that it was the name of a Greek town where one of the railroad workers was from."

http://www.usacitiesonline.com/orcountynyssa.htm#:~:text=Nyssa%20was%20founded%20in%201883,into%20a%20trading%20station%20also.

[90] "Carey is located in central Idaho at the intersection of US Highway 20 with US Highways 26 & 93. Just northeast of town is Carey Lake, and just east of Carey is Craters of the Moon National Monument. This is primarily an agricultural area, and the Blaine County Fairgrounds are here.

Carey was founded in 1883 by a group of Mormon pioneers. The town was named after Thomas Carey Stanford, younger brother of Cyrus Joseph Stanford (who was the leader of those colonists). Carey was decimated by the Great Depression and still hasn't recovered to the population levels of the early 1900's, although it has been close since the late 1970's when Carey began to evolve into one of the still-affordable bedroom communities for commuters to the Hailey-Ketchum-Sun Valley area."

http://www.sangres.com/idaho/places/blaine/carey.htm#.X6G_E4hKheU

[91] "Craters of the Moon is a vast ocean of lava flows with scattered islands of cinder cones and sagebrush."

"Craters of the Moon formed during eight major eruptive periods between 15,000 and 2000 years ago. Lava erupted from the Great Rift, a series of deep cracks that start near the visitor center and stretch 52 miles (84 km.) to the southeast."

https://www.nps.gov/crmo/

[92] "In 1955, tiny Arco won fame as the world's first nuclear-powered city. Today, it mainly serves as a jumping-off point for excursions into the nearby Craters of the Moon National Monument."

https://idaho.for91days.com/arco-and-atomic-city/

[93] "The world's first peacetime use of nuclear power occurred when the U.S. Government switched on Experimental Breeder Reactor #1 (EBR-1) near Arco, Idaho, on December 20, 1951. The town of Arco* became the first city in the world to be lit by atomic power from a reactor built near EBR-1, the BORAX III, on July 17, 1955. It was only temporary, but the way was paved for commercial use of nuclear power. The Arco reactor later suffered a partial meltdown — another World's First. There's no highway sign bragging about that."

https://www.roadsideamerica.com/story/2960

[94] "Construction began in 1949 as EBR-I became the first reactor built at the National Reactor Testing Station (NRTS), which was the original name for the 890 square miles of Idaho desert land now known as the Idaho National Laboratory (INL) Site. EBR-I is the first of 52 reactors established on the Site since 1949 as a means of researching, testing and understanding the potential of nuclear energy to bring clean power to the nation.

On Dec. 20, 1951, EBR-I successfully used nuclear fuel to light four 200-watt lightbulbs. The next day, Dec. 21, the reactor generated enough energy to light the entire building and the lights outside in the parking lot. Although this mere 400 kilowatts of power seems small by today's standards, it was absolutely monumental in the context of 1951. This was the first time a usable amount of electricity had been generated using nuclear technology, and it paved the way for an energy source of the future. As a breeder reactor, EBR-I also made more fuel than it consumed while producing electricity."

https://inl.gov/article/ebr-i-lights-up-the-history-of-nuclear-energy-development/

[95] "INL is part of the U.S. Department of Energy's complex of national laboratories. The laboratory performs work in each of the strategic goal areas of DOE: energy, national security, science and environment. INL is the nation's leading center for nuclear energy research and development."

https://inl.gov/about-inl/general-information/

[96] "The Idaho National Laboratory (INL), an 890-square-mile section of desert in southeast Idaho, was established in 1949 as the National Reactor Testing Station. Initially, the missions at the INL were the development of civilian and defense nuclear reactor technologies and management of spent nuclear fuel. Fifty-two reactors 'most of them first-of-a-kind' were built, including the Navy's first prototype nuclear propulsion plant. Of the 52 reactors, three remain in operation at the site.

In 1951, the INL achieved one of the most significant scientific accomplishments of the century - the first use of nuclear fission to produce a usable quantity of electricity at the Experimental Breeder Reactor No. 1(EBR-1). The EBR-1 is now a Registered National Historic Landmark open to the public."

https://www.id.energy.gov/insideNEID/BriefHistory.htm

[97] "Idaho Falls, city, seat (1911) of Bonneville county, southeastern Idaho, U.S., on the upper Snake River. Originally the territory of the Shoshone-Bannock and Northern Paiute Indians, it began as the Eagle Rock settlement at Taylor's Ferry (1863), later Taylor's Bridge. The town was renamed in 1890 for the low but wide (1,500 feet [460 metres]) cataract in the river (now a source of hydropower), and it developed first as a railroad division point and later as a centre of irrigated farming. The city has diversified industry, but its main sources of income are high-tech industry, agriculture (barley, potatoes), livestock, the nearby Idaho National Engineering and Environmental Laboratory (nuclear-power testing), and tourism. The Idaho Falls Mormon temple (1944) is a riverbank landmark."

https://www.britannica.com/place/Idaho-Falls

[98] https://www.nps.gov/yell/learn/nature/water.htm

[99] "Yellowstone Lake is the largest high-elevation lake (above 7,000 ft) in North America, covering up to 139 square miles, with an average depth of 138 feet, and just over 12,000,000 acre-feet of water. The lake is covered by ice from mid-December to May or June.

Entering Yellowstone Lake are more than 141 tributaries, but only one river. The Yellowstone River, which enters at the south end of the southeast arm, dominates the inflow of water and sediment flows out. The only outlet of the lake is at Fishing Bridge, where the Yellowstone River flows north and discharges 2,000–9,000 cubic feet per second."

https://www.nps.gov/yell/learn/nature/water.htm

[100] "It's easy to understand why people confuse bison and buffalo. Both are large, horned, oxlike animals of the Bovidae family. There are two kinds of bison, the American bison, and the European bison, and two forms of buffalo, water buffalo and Cape buffalo. However, it's not difficult to distinguish between them, especially if you focus on the three H's: home, hump, and horns.

Contrary to the song "Home on the Range," buffalo do not roam in the American West. Instead, they are indigenous to South Asia (water buffalo) and Africa (Cape buffalo), while bison are found in North America and parts of Europe. Despite being a misnomer—one often attributed to confused explorers—buffalo remains commonly used when referring to American bison, thus adding to the confusion."

https://www.britannica.com/story/whats-the-difference-between-buffalo-and-bison

[101] "Historic US Route 20, A Journey Across America's Longest Highway", Bryan Farr

[102] "Cody is the "Rodeo Capitol of the World. From the turn of the century, rodeos and parades have been part of the 4th of July here in Cody, Wyoming. Officially starting in 1919, the Cody Stampede rodeo has been held every summer this event established Cody as not only one of the longest running successful professional rodeos, but also the only place in the country that has a rodeo performance nightly. The Professional Rodeo Cowboy's Association named the

Cody Stampede "Best Large Outdoor Rodeo of the Year" in 1998 & 1999. In 2001 the Cody Nite Rodeo was nominated for "Best Small Outdoor Rodeo of the Year."

https://www.codystampederodeo.com/p/about/214

[103] "Thermopolis, resort town, seat (1913) of Hot Springs county, north-central Wyoming, U.S., on the Bighorn River, opposite East Thermopolis. The site was originally within the Wind River Indian Reservation (Shoshone and Arapaho). Founded in 1897, its name was derived from the Greek thermos, "hot," and polis, "city," for the nearby Big Horn Hot Springs (within present-day Hot Springs State Park), which are among the world's largest, with an outflow of 18,600,000 gallons (70,400,000 litres) a day and a water temperature of 135 °F (57 °C). Gottsche Rehabilitation Center for hot-water treatment of disease is there. A centre for livestock, grain, and sugar beets, the town is in an area of coal and sulfur mines and oil wells. The Hot Springs County Historical Museum and Cultural Center houses the "Hole-in-the-Wall" bar, visited by famous outlaws in the early 1900s. The town holds an annual Labor Day rodeo. Nearby attractions include Maytag Hot Springs and Wind River Canyon."

https://www.britannica.com/place/Thermopolis

[104] "The Wind River itself flows north through the canyon. Wind River Canyon Whitewater & Flyfishing Outfitter, a Native American-owned business, is the only outfitter permitted to raft/fish in the Indian Reservation portion of the canyon. With fallen rocks and boulders jutting from the riverbed, the unique water hydraulics make for some spectacular white water indeed.

Before it leaves the canyon, the river changes names. At the "Wedding of the Waters," the Wind River becomes the Rocky Mountain Bighorn River, named for the mountain sheep indigenous to the area. Keep an eye out for these wooly cliff dwellers as you drive. 1995 saw 43 bighorns "transplanted" along the canyon rim. After making the trip from Dubois, WY in horse trailers, the sheep were then loaded onto flatcars by Burlington-Northern Railroad before traveling the final 7 miles by railroad. They were released in the canyon, bolstering today's population to an estimated 100 sheep in Wind River Canyon."

https://travelwyoming.com/listing/shoshoni/wind-river-canyon-scenic-byway

[105] "Whether the jackalope actually exists or is simply a hoax popularized by a Douglas, Wyoming resident in 1939, is still hotly debated today.

For those who believe, the jackalope is said to be an antlered species of rabbit, sometimes rumored to be extinct. One of the rarest animals in the world, it is a cross between a now extinct pygmy-deer and a species of killer-rabbit. However, occasional sightings of this rare creature continue to occur, with small pockets of jackalope populations persisting in the American West. The antlered species of rabbit are brownish in color, weight between three and five pounds, and move with lightning speeds of up to 90 miles per hour.

They are said to be vicious when attacked and use their antlers to fight, thus they are sometimes called the "warrior rabbit."

The jackalope was first encountered by John Colter, one of the first white men to enter what would one day be the State of Wyoming."

https://www.legendsofamerica.com/wy-jackalope/

[106] UP – "The Pacific Railway Act of 1862 gave the work of building the railroad to two companies: Central Pacific, an existing California railroad, and a new railroad chartered by the Act itself – Union Pacific.

Central Pacific would start at the Pacific and head east, and Union Pacific would start in the middle of the country, the beginning of the frontier, and head west. What path Union Pacific should take was a matter of much contention. Lawmakers already realized the impact the railroad could have on local economies and wanted the business for their own states."

https://www.up.com/heritage/history/lincoln/index.htm

[107] "Through the years, a series of mergers helped Union Pacific create the strongest franchise in North America. The addition of Missouri Pacific more than doubled UP's route miles, Western Pacific track led UP to the Ports of San Francisco and Oakland, Katy gave UP access to Texas through Oklahoma, Chicago & North Western brought UP to the Twin Cities, and Southern Pacific and Denver & Rio Grande Western provided the legendary Sunset Route and a direct route through Colorado."

https://www.up.com/aboutup/special_trains/heritage/index.htm

[108] BNSF – "Few companies can claim that they've been around for a century, much less 160-plus years. And not many have had the impact on the growth of a nation that BNSF Railway and its predecessors had.

Celebrating our heritage and building on our success is one of BNSF's shared values. We are confident in our future because of the tremendous challenges we've overcome and the achievements we've made over the years. The 390 railroads that today comprise BNSF have established a great legacy for our company, which became part of the Berkshire Hathaway family in 2010.

While many different railroads combined to form BNSF, the people who worked at those railroads shared many traits. We were — and continue to be — a unique breed, blending visionary thinking with the pragmatism of results-oriented business leaders."

https://www.bnsf.com/bnsf-resources/pdf/about-bnsf/History_and_Legacy.pdf

[109] "Frank S. Lusk was born April 27, 1857. He came to Wyoming for the first time in 1877 but only stayed for a short time. His travels took him to numerous states but in 1880 he returned and purchased land that would later become the town site of Lusk, Wyoming. After purchasing and establishing his land, he decided to put in for a post office on the land rather than travel to the closest one located at Rawhide Buttes. The post office was given the name 'Lusk' which then named the town Lusk and has since never been changed. In 1894 Frank S. Lusk married Louise B. (Findley) Lusk. Together, they resided for a time in the town of Lusk with their adopted daughter Vivian Gorham Lusk (Mahmood Abozeid) before leaving the town. In 1930 Frank S. Lusk died in Missoula, Montana on August 6."

https://www.townoflusk.org/

[110] John Koster writes:

"Just who killed the Lakota fighting man remains in dispute.

The scenario is familiar: Crazy Horse, greatest war chief of the Lakota Nation, harasser of George Crook and destroyer of George Custer, struggles to avoid being shut in the guardhouse at Camp Robinson, Nebraska, and is bayoneted by a soldier. Books and movies have depicted Crazy Horse's demise—but there is a lot of room for debate and a very good chance it did not happen that way.

The circumstances of Crazy Horse's arrest, while complicated, are not in serious doubt. He surrendered his weapons to the United States on May 6, 1877, so his people wouldn't starve to death. Then, in August, the U.S. Army asked Crazy Horse to take up arms again and help subdue Chief Joseph's Nez Perces, who had broken out of custody to avoid being deported from their homeland. Sarcastically—and probably with an escape of his own in mind—Crazy Horse told his captors that he would fight until not a Nez Perce was left. Frank Grouard, an interpreter who disliked Crazy Horse, twisted the Lakota chief's words to suggest he would fight until not a white man was left.

Faced with this menacing but almost certainly false translation, General Crook condoned the arrest of Crazy Horse and left the post, possibly to avoid what might happen next. The commander of Camp Robinson, Lt. Col. Luther P. Bradley, dispatched Captain Daniel Burke to negotiate with the Indian agent for the Brulé Sioux (Sicangu Lakota), Jesse Lee, a former Army lieutenant who knew Crazy Horse as a friend and had invited him to sit-down dinners with his family. Crazy Horse was a nephew of Chief Spotted Tail, and Burke promised both Spotted Tail and the agent that Crazy Horse would be well treated if he left all weapons and came in for a peaceful talk. The idea that the government already had plans to ship Crazy Horse to the Dry Tortugas off the Florida coast, last stop on earth for many warriors, is controversial. But the Army had no intention of releasing Crazy Horse after his "threat against Americans." Accounts vary as to whether he was to be shipped to Omaha, Cheyenne or the Tortugas.

Handling arrangements at Camp Robinson on September 5, 1877, was Lieutenant William Philo Clark, known as "White Hat" to the Lakotas, an Indian sign language expert and Crook's right-hand man in Indian matters. Lee had sent notice that Crazy Horse was coming into camp with a handful of other now-peaceful Indians and had been told to arrive unarmed and to expect good treatment—although the warrior himself had been plagued with foreboding. In fact, when the party arrived at the camp, Clark told Lee that Crazy Horse would be handed over to the officer of the day, a euphemism for detention.

When Crazy Horse, surrounded by soldiers and Indian agency police, saw the guardhouse and realized what was happening, a struggle broke out, during which the chief was mortally wounded. Crazy Horse died about midnight. The Army gave his body to his grieving parents, who buried him in an unknown location —possibly near Wounded Knee Creek."

https://www.historynet.com/death-crazy-horse-fables-forensics.htm

[111] Fall River in Hot Springs, South Dakota

"Called Minnekahta (warm waters) by the original white settlers in 1879, the town's name was changed to Hot Springs in 1886. Earlier, the Lakota and the Cheyenne Indian tribes fought for control of the natural warm waters. Legends tell of a hostile encounter waged in the hills high above the gurgling springs on a peak called Battle Mountain.

Spurred by a vast range and tall grass, ranchers staked their bankroll on cattle and helped build the town of Hot Springs. Merchants sold their wares, and by 1890 local residents such as businessman Fred Evans and others of entrepreneurial spirit embarked on an ambitious plan to turn the whole town into a health spa. Evans built the Evans Plunge over a group of small springs and one giant thermal spout of warm mineral water.

When the railroad began unloading passengers at the Hot Springs Train Depot in 1891, the town's future was secured. From the mineral water's mist rose elaborate sandstone buildings, and proprietors provided all manner of services and goods."

https://www.hotsprings-sd.com/discover-hot-springs/history/

[112] "Although there were French fur trappers and traders in the Custer area by 1796, there was no town of Custer until August 10, 1875. On that date General George Crook persuaded the miners illegally in the area to leave until the Black Hills became opened to white settlement. Crook allowed the assembled miners to lay out and name a town and allowed seven men to remain in the area to protect their mining claims.

Thomas Hooper laid out the town one mile square with a picket rope and a pocket compass. Lots were numbered and the miners present drew for the lot they could claim when the area would be opened for settlement.

When it came to naming the town, veterans of the Civil War who had served in the Union Army suggested the name of Custer to honor the general who had made a reputation for himself. Veterans of the Confederate Army suggested the town to be named Stonewall in honor of their Civil War hero, Stonewall Jackson. A vote was taken to decide the matter. There being more Union veterans than Confederate veterans—although the number was close to half and half—the name of Custer won."

https://custer.govoffice.com/history

[113] Crazy Horse Mountain and the start of the carving

https://crazyhorsememorial.org/story/the-mountain

[114] "Getting this project underway was a challenge all by itself. Once Doane Robinson and others had found a sculptor, Gutzon Borglum, they had to get permission to do the carving. Senator Peter Norbeck and Congressman William Williamson were instrumental in getting the legislation passed to allow the carving. Williamson drafted two bills, one each to be introduced in the United States Congress and the South Dakota Legislature. The bill requesting permission to use federal land for the memorial easily passed through Congress. The bill sent to the South Dakota Legislature faced more opposition. The Mount Harney National Memorial bill was defeated twice before narrowly passing. Governor Gunderson signed the bill on March 5, 1925 and established the Mount Harney Memorial

Association later that summer.

Early in the project, money was hard to find, despite Borglum's promise that eastern businessmen would gladly make large donations. He also promised the citizens of South Dakota that they would not be responsible for paying for any of the mountain carving. In the summer of 1927, President Calvin Coolidge was in the Black Hills and Borglum was planning a formal dedication of the mountain. Borglum hired a plane to fly over the State Game Lodge in Custer State Park where Coolidge was staying. As he flew over, Borglum dropped a wreath to invite the President to the dedication ceremony. President Coolidge agreed to attend the ceremony, which was held on August 10, 1927, and gave a speech promising federal funding for the project."

https://www.nps.gov/moru/learn/historyculture/memorial-history.htm

[115] https://www.lightofmineranch.com/

[116] "Cherry County is the largest county located in the state of Nebraska. The population is about 5,713. Its county seat is Valentine. The county was named for Lt. Samuel A. Cherry, an Army officer who was stationed at Fort Niobrara and who had been killed in South Dakota in 1881. Cherry County is nestled among the beautiful rolling Nebraska Sandhills."

https://visitvalentine.org/history-culture/

[117] "O'Neill, county seat of Holt County, was founded by General John O'Neill, a native of Ireland and veteran of the American Civil War. The "general," a rank bestowed on him by admirers because he commanded three Fenian incursions into British-governed Canada, first directed colonists in 1874 to this fertile Elkhorn Valley site which bears his name. General O'Neill also induced other Irish groups to settle at Atkinson in Holt County and in Greeley County.

Many Irish coming to O'Neill had emigrated to America earlier, as result of famine and economic distress, temporarily settling in eastern cities. General O'Neill, knowing the agricultural heritage of his people, said his object in founding Nebraska colonies was "to encourage poor people in getting away from the overcrowded cities of the East."

The Irish were a major immigrant group contributing to the settlement of Nebraska. Speaking the English language, they blended into the population and were found in many communities. However, due to ancient animosities with Britain, some of them colonized in America. Foremost colony in this state is O'Neill, proclaimed the Irish Capital of Nebraska by the Governor in 1969."

http://www.cityofoneillnebraska.com/history-of-o-neill.html

[118] "Welcome to the Basilica of St. Francis Xavier! Our church has been a Catholic treasure among the cornfields of Iowa for over 125 years, welcoming visitors to an experience of both beauty and prayer. We invite you to come and visit, to pray, to join us at Mass, and to appreciate with us the Catholic heritage we love and celebrate. To the greater glory and honor of God!"

http://xavierbasilica.com/

[119] "The DeSoto House began its years as the center of Galena's social and political activities. The most notable visitor was President Abraham Lincoln, who spoke from its Main Street balcony on July 23, 1856, in support of John Fremont's bid for the presidency. Just two years later, on July 25, 1858 Senator Stephen A. Douglas spoke from the same balcony. On September 13, 1860, a crowd of over 15,000 rallied in front of the DeSoto in response to a "Grand Republican Mass Meeting" in support of Lincoln's presidential bid. Ulysses S. Grant's return to his hometown of Galena following the Civil War, brought 25,000 citizens to the streets to welcome him home. Bands, parades, and cannon salutes preceded a reception ball for 2,000 persons which was held at the DeSoto House. Grant later used rooms 209 and 211 of the hotel as his presidential campaign headquarters."

https://www.visitgalena.org/Venue/DeSoto-House-Hotel

[120] "Chicago is the most important railroad center in North America. More lines of track radiate in more directions from Chicago than from any other city. Chicago has long been the most important interchange point for freight traffic between the nation's major railroads and it is the hub of Amtrak, the intercity rail passenger system. Chicago ranks

second (behind New York City) in terms of the volume of commuter rail passengers carried each day.

The first railroad in Chicago was the Galena & Chicago Union, which was chartered in 1836 to build tracks to the lead mines at Galena in northwestern Illinois. The first tracks were laid in 1848, and then not to Galena but to a point known as Oak Ridge (now Oak Park). The Galena & Chicago Union's terminal stood near the corner of Canal and Kinzie Streets."

http://www.encyclopedia.chicagohistory.org/pages/1039.html

[121] "Illinois Harley-Davidson® can trace its history all the way back to 1916, when Wilbur "Bill" H. Thede opened his first motorcycle dealership on Lake Street in Melrose Park, IL. In 1925, Thede, known then as "The Motorcycle Man", became one of the first Harley-Davidson® dealers in the Chicago area. In addition to Harley-Davidson® motorcycles, sidecars, and package trucks, Thede sold bicycles, Johnson marine engines, and various British cycles. In 1938, Thede moved Illinois Harley-Davidson® to a larger, three-story building in Oak Park, IL.

When the war ended in 1945, Thede moved the dealership again, this time to a storefront at 7577 W. Lake Street in River Forest. The dealership continued to prosper, and by 1962 Thede made the move back to Oak Park, this time to 6510 W. Roosevelt Road.

In 1967, Bob Maxant and his father Bob Maxant Sr. purchased Illinois Harley-Davidson® from Mr. Thede. The purchase included the Oak Park dealership, two Electra Glides®, one Sportster® and a total of nineteen lightweight Sprints and Rapidos, manufactured by Aermacchi. Illinois Harley-Davidson®'s only employee, Jerry Kiesow, also came with the deal to help Bob and Senior, manage their new dealership. Jerry was a mechanic, partsman and salesman, all-in-one. Today, we're part of the Windy City Group and proudly serve the motorcycle communities of Chicago, Burbank, Oak Park, Oak Lawn, and Westmont, IL.

In 2011, current Owners Ozzie & Jill Giglio purchased Oak Lawn Harley-Davidson® from Neal Houbolt and Illinois Harley-Davidson® from Bob Maxant. They merged and work closely with both family's in order to retain the historic legacy's of both Oak Lawn Harley-Davidson® and Illinois Harley-Davidson®, two of Chicagoland's legacies and favorite stores for Harley-Davidson® riders to visit. The classic motorcycles on display date back to 1910. Vast amount of vintage memorabilia and photographs are showcased throughout the dealership. Illinois Harley-Davidson® has prevailed and premiered throughout the decades as a leading dealership serving thousands of riders throughout Chicagoland area and those traveling on the "Mother Road" Route 66."

https://www.illinoishd.com/

[122] "There's no doubt about it – visitors to Indiana's Cool North love everything Amish. The scrumptious food, intricate hand-stitched quilts, finely crafted furniture, the ever-present horse-drawn buggies, and the quiet farmsteads are truly captivating. There are many ways to get to know the Amish people, who live a lifestyle of simplicity, foregoing modern amenities such as electricity, cars, and telephones. Here's a guide for immersing yourself in all things Amish in Northern Indiana's Elkhart and LaGrange counties – home to some 23,000 Amish residents, one of the largest Amish population in the nation."

https://www.indianascoolnorth.com/things-to-do/arts-entertainment/discover-the-fascinating-world-of-the-amish-in-northern-indiana/

[123] "The Amish and Mennonite groups emerged from the Anabaptist movement during the 16th-century Protestant Reformation in Central and Western Europe. To escape persecution, the Dutch Anabaptist leader and former Catholic priest Menno Simons gathered his followers and fled to Switzerland, where the Mennonite group was established. By the end of the 17th century, a group led by Jakob Amman split from the Swiss Mennonite group and was named Amish after its leader.

Attracted by the promise of religious freedom, the Amish began migrating to Pennsylvania in the early 1700s. Amish residents, who first settled in this area near Middlebury in 1841, are descendants of the Swiss Amish from Pennsylvania."

https://www.visitelkhartcounty.com/plan/area-info/amish-culture/

[124] "The most popular landmark in Angola is the Monument, referred to by locals as "The Mound" or the 'Circle.'

Built in 1917 by E.M. Heltzer, The Monument commemorates the Civil War. It has statues for all four branches of the military. On top is the statue of Columbia, facing east. It cost $17,000 in 1917, over $1,000,000 if it were built today. The Monument is the center of many town celebrations and festivities. It was unveiled on Thursday, September 13, 1917 at 1PM to much fanfare. On the Monument are plaques with the names of the 1,278 men from Steuben County who fought in the war. Per capita, more men from Steuben County enlisted for the war than any other county in Indiana. The monument underwent a renovation in 1993 and was re-dedicated during Fourth of July ceremonies."

https://www.angolain.org/category/?categoryid=9

[125] "Cleveland was the first settlement founded in the Connecticut Western Reserve by the Connecticut Land Company. It was named after General Moses Cleaveland, an investor in the company who led the survey of its land within the Western Reserve. The town was located along the eastern bank of the Cuyahoga River. On January 6, 1831, the Cleveland Advertiser dropped the "a" from Cleveland, probably to save space on the newspaper's masthead, thus the spelling we use today. The first survey of Cleveland was completed in 1796, and it included 220 lots. The company originally charged fifty dollars for lots in the settlement and found that few people were willing to pay that much to live there. As late as 1800, a company representative reported that only three men lived in Cleveland. Ten years later, there were only fifty-seven residents. Despite its small population, Cleveland became the Cuyahoga County seat in 1807."

http://ohiohistorycentral.org/w/Cleveland,_Ohio

[126] "The world's first electric traffic signal is put into place on the corner of Euclid Avenue and East 105th Street in Cleveland, Ohio, on August 5, 1914."

https://www.history.com/this-day-in-history/first-electric-traffic-signal-installed

[127] "It was near the mouth of Conneaut Creek, a stream not then navigable, but now one of the deepest and most important harbors on the south shore of Lake Erie that Moses Cleaveland and his party of surveyors first touched Ohio, in their journey to this section for purpose of making a survey of the Western Reserve, the new possession of the Connecticut Land Company, of Connecticut."

"Conneaut - The following is taken from the News Herald:

"The name of Conneaut was given to the stream bordering our city by a tribe of Seneca Indians and signifies "River of Many Fish."

"Arriving at the mouth of Conneaut River, July 4, 1796, a group of 50 surveyors under Moses Cleaveland named the point of land on which they touched "Fort Independence".

"In the fall of the same year came the first settlers, James Kingsbury and family. He had one child, the first to be born on Western Reserve territory, which included what is now Ohio.

"The year 1789 saw the first permanent settlement. These pioneers consisted of Thomas Montgomery and wife and Aaron Wright.

"The following year found several other settlements started along the creek and in the closely succeeding years many other families arrived.

"Conneaut Township was organized in 1804 and born the name of "Salem" until 1832, when the name was changed to "Conneaut."

"The year 1832 saw the publication of the first journal in Conneaut, called the "Ashtabula County Gazette.""

http://www.conneautohio.us/Ashtaco_ConneautHistory_xviii.htm

[128] "The Township of Girard was carved out of Elk Creek, Fairview and Springfield in 1832, receiving its name from Stephen Girard, the Philadelphia millionaire, who owned a large body of land in the adjoining township of Conneaut, on which he had arranged just before his death to put up mills and make other important improvements which were expected to benefit the whole country around."

https://www.girardtownship.com/about

[129] The Town of North East, Pennsylvania

"In 1869 the South Shore Wine Co. was formed, and several other wineries soon followed. Today, the North East area boasts eleven thriving wineries, thousands of acres of vineyards and two large fruit processing plants."

https://nechamber.org/about-north-east/

[130] "Ripley's first settler to purchase land was Alexander Cochran. He arrived from Ireland in 1802, and made his land purchase official two years later. His fifth generation descendant, A. James Cochrane (whose grandfather added the "e"), still owns some of the original acreage.

In 1816 the largest concentration of population in this area was established as a town and named Quincy. By 1873 it was known as Ripley, named for Gen. Eleazar Wheelock Ripley, active in the War of 1812. The township grew slowly until the opening of the Erie Canal in 1825 and it became more accessible. One famous visitor about that time was the Marquis de Lafayette, on his way from Erie, PA, to Portland, NY. Many other nameless visitors came as the Underground Railway conductors brought escaping slaves to Ripley's shoreline, just 25 miles from Canada."

http://www.ripley-ny.com/about-ripley/history

[131] "Westfield is home to the Westfield Republican, the first Republican newspaper established soon after the Republican Party formed in 1854. Westfield also was the home of Grace Bedell, a young girl who changed the face of the 1860 Presidential campaign, or, more accurately changed the face of Republican candidate Abraham Lincoln. Grace went to see Candidate Lincoln at a campaign stop and later sent him a pithy letter suggesting that he could garner more votes by growing whiskers. Lincoln took the message to heart and began to grow a beard immediately and just a few weeks later won the election. President-Elect Lincoln later stopped in Westfield and specifically asked to meet the young lady who had advised him to grow whiskers. Their meeting is depicted in statues adorning a small park in the Village of Westfield."

https://westfieldny.com/living-here/history

[132] "On March 20, 1894, between the hours of 10 a.m. and 3 p.m., in the rooms of the Brocton Library on Fay Street, 187 persons voted on the question of whether or not to incorporate Brocton.

The result was 127 yes, 60 no. The Village of Brocton was born."

"Incorporation of Brocton came almost 83 years after Elijah Fay, formerly of Southborough, Mass., purchased all of lot 20 which formed the west portion of the Village of Brocton and built a log cabin. His brother, Hollis, in 1813, cleared three or four acres and built a log cabin on the northwest part of lot 13 which was the east section of Brocton."

https://www.brocton.org/history.php

[133] "The Village of Silver Creek is located on the shores of Lake Erie, within the Town of Hanover, Chautauqua County, New York, in an area of Western New York known as the Concord Grape Belt."

http://silvercreekny.com/

[134] "An Introduction To Geneva's History

The first mention of the settlement called by the name "Geneva" occurs in 1788, though we are left with no record of why that name was chosen. Geneva was the strategic center of Western NY. The area which became the village and later the city of Geneva was fertile, fruitful, and inhabited first by the Algonquin then later by the Seneca Nation, members of the Haudenosaunee Confederacy. The northwest corner of the shore of Seneca Lake was used as a military outpost by British Loyalists in the persons of Col. John Butler's Rangers. Settlers began to move in after 1792 when the Pulteney Associates hired Charles Williamson as their land agent to promote the development of the area.

Farmers from other areas where land was not as fertile as that in Geneva began to migrate to Geneva from New England, Maryland, Virginia, eastern New York, and Pennsylvania. The population of the Genesee Country, the land area bounded by Seneca Lake on the east, the Genesee River on the west, the Pennsylvania border on the south and Lake Ontario on the north grew from a population of 1,000 in 1791 to 30,000 in 1810. The Village of Geneva grew with them. Geneva was incorporated as a village in 1806 and a city in 1897."

http://cityofgenevany.com/the-history-of-geneva/

[135] "In the spring of 1779, George Washington faced a dilemma.

While his Continental Army kept watch over the main British force based in New York City, he was forced to deal with the Indian and Tory threat to his rear.

On July 3, 1778, an enemy force of approximately 1,000 Iroquois and Tories under the command of Major John Butler culminated a summer of terror along the North Branch of the Susquehanna River with an assault on the fertile Wyoming Valley. The Wyoming Valley Massacre claimed an estimated 160 to 320 lives

Washington's solution was to split his force, sending nearly a third of his tiny army on a punitive raid into Iroquois country.

The expedition, under the command of Gen. John Sullivan, left its mark on Wyoming and Bradford counties as well as the Finger Lakes region where the force waged a scorched-earth attack against the Iroquois homeland.

Sullivan's March began in Wilkes-Barre on July 31, 1779"

https://sites.rootsweb.com/~pasulliv/Sullivans.htm

[136] "The story of Waterloo begins with the Cayuga Indian village of Skoi-Yase, established about the year 1500, and located near the rapids of the Seneca River, near the present location of Locust Street in Waterloo. The Cayugas valued Skoi-Yase, meaning "flowing water" because of the abundant supply of fish, especially eels, in the Seneca River. Many great Indian councils were held at Skoi-Yase; the national Indian leaders Red Jacket and Chief Corn Planter attended some of the deliberative sessions."

http://waterloony.com/about-us/history-of-waterloo/

[137] "Early Waterloo was a thriving industrial village. Historical events of national importance have occurred here and given birth to many "firsts." Much of the planning for the first Woman's Rights Convention held in Seneca Falls, NY in 1848, took place in Waterloo at the Hunt and McClintock houses. The most significant Waterloo first is the birth of Memorial Day. On May 5, 1866, Waterloo conducted the nation's first formal, continuing remembrance of veterans who had died in war. The Federal Government in 1966 formally recognized Waterloo as the Birthplace of Memorial Day. The Mormon religion had its birth on the Peter Whitmer farm two miles south of Waterloo and tile drainage in America was originated by John Johnston on his farm a few miles west of this village. The first Pullman car was conceived and constructed by a Waterloo man, Major Frederick Furniss. In the 1890's, funeral directors Mr. Genung of Waterloo and Mr. Eckels of Philadelphia developed the first modern method of embalming."

http://waterloony.com/about-us/history-of-waterloo/

[138] "The first white settlers along the Seneca River arrived in the area in the late 18th century. They were part of Sullivan's March and had seen the potential the area held. Water played an important part in the development of the area. Seneca County, when erected March 24, 1804, originally covered an area extending from the shore of Lake Ontario to just south of Ithaca; a distance of about 63 miles north to south and 11 miles east to west. It was divided into 6 towns: Junius, Fayette, Romulus, Ovid, Hector and Ulysses."

http://www.senecafalls.com/history.php

[139] "Seneca Falls was also gaining a reputation for social and religious reform. Abolition of Slavery and the Underground Railroad, the Temperance movement and women's rights were among issues supported by local residents. On July 19 and 20, 1848 the first Convention on Women's Rights was held at the Wesleyan Chapel on Fall Street in Seneca Falls. Organized by Jane Hunt, Elizabeth Cady Stanton, Mary Ann M'Clintock and others, it was the birth of the Women's Rights Movement."

http://www.senecafalls.com/history.php

[140] "Seneca Falls is widely believed to be the inspiration for Frank Capra's holiday classic, "It's A Wonderful Life". Come to Seneca Falls and visit the village and locations that inspired Mr. Capra in his visits to Seneca Falls in the early 1900's."

https://www.senecafalls.com/visit-seneca-falls.php

[141] "The Diocese of Rochester was established by the Vatican on January 24, 1868 with the appointment of the Rev. Bernard J. McQuaid of Newark, New Jersey as its first bishop.

One of the first acts of the new bishop was the division of Holy Family parish in Auburn and the announcement of a new parish, which was to lie west of State Street and the Owasco River. The new parish was organized on August 15, 1868 and called ST. MARY OF THE ASSUMPTION, in honor of the feast of the day.

In August of 1868, the Rev. Thomas A. Maher, the first pastor of St. Mary's parish, came to Auburn and rented a house at 34 State St. where he celebrated Mass. He later made use of Tallman Hall at the corner of State and Dill streets. Records tell us that the following notice was published in the Auburn Daily Advertiser on September 12, 1868: "St. Mary's (new) Catholic Church service Sunday, September 13, 1868 at Brown's Commercial College…" A certificate of incorporation was issued to Father Maher, pastor, and Michael Kavanaugh and Patrick Kelly, trustees, on September 26, 1868."

https://www.stmaryauburn.org/about-us/history-of-parish/

[142] "The Underground Railroad (UR) reached its height between 1850 and 1860. The passage of the Fugitive Slave Act in 1850 made it more dangerous for those who helped slaves escape or offered them shelter. The consequence could be jail or a hefty fine."

http://www.harriet-tubman.org/supporters-of-the-underground-railroad/

[143] "In 1858 New York Senator William Seaward made Harriet Tubman a proposition. He would sell her his property in Auburn, NY for a reasonable price and flexible terms. Auburn had a strong abolitionist group and Seaward was a well known supporter of the Underground Railroad who Harriet could depend on for funds and shelter for her people. Before the Civil War about 500 slaves passed through Auburn on their way north. Tubman knew Senator Seaward well as she had used his house as a station many times. She was encouraged to move to Auburn by a long time friend and supporter, Lucretia Mott.

Tubman had been living in North Street in St. Catharines, Ontario, Canada West since 1851; that was her home and her base of operation. She had brought her parents and her entire family to St. Catharines where they lived safe from slave catchers. But Tubman could not resist the offer and in 1858 Tubman and Senator Seaward sealed the deal for $1,200."

http://www.harriet-tubman.org/house/

[144] "Founded in 1793 by John Lincklaen, Cazenovia resides on the Southeast shore of Cazenovia lake. The village of Cazenovia is located on U.S. Route 20, an East–West United States highway that stretches 3,365 mi from New England all the way to the Pacific Northwest, and is the home to many quaint shops, restaurants, lodging, history, and more!"

https://cazenovia.com/

[145] https://daves-diner-diner.business.site/

[146] "Cazenovia College traces its birth to 1824, when it was founded as the Seminary of the Genesee Conference, the second Methodist seminary to be established in the United States. It opened in what had been the Madison County Courthouse."

https://www.cazenovia.edu/about/history-cazenovia-college

[147] "The first settlers in the area of Morrisville came from the east by way of the "Old State Road" which passed through the village about where Eaton and Maple Streets cross. Thomas Morris came here in 1796 and in 1797 built a house on the corner of Main and Cedar Streets.

As more people came to the area, a small village grew and was called "Morris Flats" after the founder. The Cherry Valley Turnpike [*] brought in more settlers, but "The Flats" did not progress as fast as "Log City" (the early name of the hamlet of Eaton) until after the county seat was moved here in 1817. At that time the village was still a small hamlet."

https://www.morrisvilleny.com/history/

* The Cherry Valley Turnpike from Albany to Manlius eventually became the route that US 20 followed between Albany and Cazenovia as it passed through Morrisville.

[148] "Richfield Springs is a village in the town of Richfield in Otsego County. It's located along Route 20, 65 miles west of Albany and 65 miles east of Syracuse. Once a popular resort town, it was home to grand hotels and guest houses. Seven trains of visitors arrived daily to enjoy the health benefits of Richfield's sulfur springs."

https://www.newyorkupstate.com/entertainment/erry-2018/05/5b76b17f2e9017/a_day_in_richfield_springs_pho.html

[149] https://www.thisiscooperstown.com/town/richfield-springs

[150] https://www.trainorders.com/discussion/read.php?2,1957490

[151] "The majority of Bishop McCloskey's immigrant Irish flock came to America from Ireland during the harrowing Potato Famine. Being poor and uneducated, they became the object of much ridicule and scorn from the Yankee establishment. The "Know Nothing Movement" at the time was strong in its attacks on immigrants, especially Catholics. Bishop McCloskey realized that his first task was to help Catholics take their rightful place in their new country. One way for this to be done was by building a great cathedral of which all could be proud. Bishop McCloskey commissioned a young Irish architect, Patrick Charles Keely, (1816-1896) of Brooklyn, New York, to design and build Albany's Cathedral. Keely emigrated to New York in 1842 at age 26."

https://cathedralic.com/history/

[152] "As the last surviving Major General of the Revolutionary War, Lafayette was invited by U.S. president James Monroe and Congress to visit the 24-state Union for what would become his Farewell Tour in the United States of America. Accompanied by his Secretary Auguste Levasseur, General Lafayette visited all the 24 states of the Union in 13 months (August 1824 – September 1825)."

"The Lafayette Trail is an effort spearheaded by the American Friends of Lafayette and the Consulate of France in Boston to memorialize the footsteps of General Lafayette during his momentous tour in 1824-1825 in preparation for the Bicentennial of the Farewell Tour in 2024. Currently focused on the New England portion of the tour, the Lafayette Trail is poised to expand west and south to encompass all of the 24 states that Lafayette visited during his tour."

https://www.battlefields.org/learn/articles/lafayette-trail-mapping-general-lafayettes-farewell-tour-united-states-1824-1825

[153] "Ironically, Col. Jacob Wendell, the man credited with initiating and guiding the original settlement of Pittsfield, never lived here and may have never even visited. In 1738, the wealthy Bostonian bought 24,000 acres of lands known originally as Pontoosuck, a Mohican Indian word meaning "a field or haven for winter deer," as a speculative investment, which he planned to subdivide and resell to others who would settle here. He formed a partnership with Philip Livingston, a wealthy kinsman from Albany, and Col. John Stoddard of Northampton, who already had claim to 1,000 acres here.

A group of young men came and began to clear the land in 1743, but threats of Indian raids associated with the conflict of the French and Indian wars soon forced them to leave, and the land remained unoccupied by those of European descent for several more years. Finally, in 1752, settlers, many from Westfield, Massachusetts, arrived and a village began to grow, which was incorporated as Pontoosuck Plantation in 1753. By 1761 there were 200 residents, and the plantation became the Township of Pittsfield, named in honor of British Prime Minister William Pitt, who later would champion the colonists' cause before the revolution."

https://www.cityofpittsfield.org/residents/history_of_pittsfield/index.php

[154] http://historicus20.com/visitor.html

[155] "Huntington has a colorful history, hinted at by the town's incorporation date of 1855, decades later than the towns around it. The town was assembled from pieces of surrounding towns, which were grafted onto the town of Norwich.

The present village center sits on what was the meeting point of three towns and two counties. The location of the village created a tangle of jurisdictional confusion. With the coming of the railroad in the 1840's and the expansion of industry and population that came with it, the political difficulties that the boundaries presented became untenable.

The solution that resulted in the town we call home today was crafted by a Northampton attorney named Charles Huntington. Once it was incorporated, Mr. Huntington presented the new town with a gift that was the foundation of the town's library. After some discussion, the newly-formed town voted to adopt the of name of 'Huntington', in honor of its recent architect and benefactor."

https://huntingtonma.us/history.html

[156] "In August 1909, Mr. Edwin A. Grozier, Publisher of the Boston Post, a newspaper, forwarded to the Board of Selectmen in 700 towns* (no cities included) in New England a gold-headed ebony cane with the request that it be presented with the compliments of the Boston Post to the oldest male citizen of the town, to be used by him as long as he lives (or moves from the town), and at his death handed down to the next oldest citizen of the town.

The cane would belong to the town and not the man who received it. The canes were all made by J.F. Fradley and Co., a New York manufacturer, from ebony shipped in seven-foot lengths from the Congo in Africa. They were cut to cane lengths, seasoned for six months, turned on lathes to the right thickness, coated and polished. They had a 14-carat gold head two inches long, decorated by hand, and a ferrule tip. The head was engraved with the inscription, —- Presented by the Boston Post to the oldest citizen of (name of the town) —- "To Be Transmitted." "

https://www.townofcharlton.net/229/Boston-Post-Cane-Committee

[157] "The Town of Oxford is located in Worcester County, Massachusetts, approximately 11 miles south of Worcester, MA. Oxford is the birthplace of Clara Barton, the founder of the American Red Cross. Oxford is also the birthplace of Elliot Joslin, the first doctor in the United States to specialize in diabetes and founder of today's Joslin Diabetes Center."

https://www.town.oxford.ma.us/about-us

[158] "Worcester named after Worcester, England was first established as a town in 1722 and later became a city in 1848. During the past three centuries Worcester has evolved from its modest, but instrumental revolutionary beginnings to a major manufacturing center to its current concentration of world-class colleges and universities, medical facilities and teaching hospitals."

http://www.worcesterma.gov/city-clerk/worcester-history

[159] "Worcester is located in Central Massachusetts, and is known as the "heart of the Commonwealth." Worcester was established as a town on June 14, 1722, chosen the shire town or county seat of Worcester County in 1731, and incorporated as a city on February 29, 1848."

http://www.worcesterhistory.org/worcesters-history/

[160] "Ross Wyman, a blacksmith, was a member of Shrewsbury's Committees of Correspondence, Safety and Inspection, and the town's only gunsmith. During the American Revolution, the Committees of Correspondence, Safety and Inspection were three different local committees of patriots that operated as a shadow government – they took control of the thirteen colonies away from royal officials, who became increasingly helpless.

Ross was one of Shrewsbury's minutemen and a Captain of the local artillery company. He was attached to Colonel Jonathan Ward's regiment, which marched to Cambridge on the alarm of April 19, 1775. It was in Cambridge that General Artemas Ward, also of Shrewsbury, established his headquarters."

https://www.shrewsburyhistoricalsociety.org/gunsmithing

[161] "The Town of Northborough, originally part of the Town of Marlborough, then Westborough, was incorporated in 1766 and became a full-fledged town with the right of representation at the Great and General Court of Boston in 1775. The early churches of Massachusetts, called "meeting houses," were the center of all town activity. Built on land given by Capt. James Eager, Northborough's first Meeting House stood about where the First Congregational Unitarian Church is today, on Church Street."

https://www.town.northborough.ma.us/about-northborough-ma

[162] "Wayland was the first settlement of the Sudbury plantation, established in 1638, and incorporated in 1639. Among the 60 original men, women, and children, were 15 Puritan families who had traveled in the ship Confidence from England. These original families included the Curtis's, Grouts, Stones, Haynes, Noyes, Bents, and Goodenows. Bringing with them the English pattern of farming, with collective fields and grazing along with individual lots, they named their town Sudbury after the town in Suffolk, where their pastor Edmund Brown and some of their company had lived. The original settlement was clustered one half mile northwest of the present town center, now Bow and Old Sudbury road. The abundant pasturage along the Sudbury River that attracted them is evident today at the town's Cow Common conservation area and extensive Great Meadows National Wildlife Refuge areas. Wayland and Sudbury residents established the Sudbury Valley Trust in 1953 in part to protect these lands. Today Wayland is in the top 5 communities in the state in conservation acreage."

https://www.wayland.ma.us/about-us/pages/puritan-village-1638

[163] Waltham has a long history and, for those interested, a timeline can be found at this site.

https://www.waltham-community.com/history.html

[164] "Waltham, city, Middlesex county, eastern Massachusetts, U.S., on the Charles River, just west of Boston. Settled in the 1630s, it was part of Watertown until separately incorporated in 1738. Abundant waterpower attracted early gristmills and paper mills. In 1813 the first textile mill for processing raw cotton into finished cloth under one roof was established there. Industrialization followed, and the American Waltham Watch Company (founded 1854) became the nation's first mass-producer of watches. Until the mid-20th century, it was one of the world's largest and played an important role in the city's progress."

https://www.britannica.com/place/Waltham

[165] "According to the Hotel Buckminster's website, the hotel was where the Black Sox scandal all began, a Major League Baseball game-fixing scandal in which eight members of the Chicago White Sox were accused of throwing the 1919 World Series against the Cincinnati Reds in exchange for money from a gambling syndicate."

https://www.bostonherald.com/2020/04/07/historic-hotel-buckminster-in-bostons-kenmore-square-closes-due-to-coronavirus/

[166] "The city of Hartford, located in Hartford County and a part of central Connecticut, is the state's capital and often goes by the nickname the Insurance Capital of the World. First settled in 1635 by Thomas Hooker, John Haynes, and a group of 100 followers from the Massachusetts Bay Colony, it is one of the oldest towns in the state. Over time, Hartford grew to be one of the most prosperous cities in the nation, and by the late-19th century, was the wealthiest city in the country. Today, Hartford is known for the Colt Manufacturing Company, the city's ties to Mark Twain and the Stowe family, and for its critical role in the evolution of the state."

https://connecticuthistory.org/towns-page/hartford/#:~:text=First%20settled%20in%201635%20by,wealthiest%20city%20in%20the%20country.

[167] "Samuel Colt, the man who revolutionized firearms manufacturing in the United States, was born in Hartford, Connecticut, on July 19, 1814. The son of a textile worker, Colt got himself expelled from Amherst Academy as a young man, so his father sent him on a year-long sailing voyage to study navigation. While aboard ship, Colt became enamored with the spinning and locking mechanisms used by the ship's wheel and carved a wooden model of a revolver that used a similar mechanism for loading and firing ammunition."

https://connecticuthistory.org/the-colt-patent-fire-arms-manufacturing-company/

[168] "Missouri-born Samuel Clemens is best known by his pen name Mark Twain. The author, lecturer, humorist, and sometime inventor moved to Hartford in 1871, shortly after marrying Olivia Langdon. There, in the Nook Farm area inhabited by literary talents, social reformers, and other accomplished individuals, the couple built a home that is today the Mark Twain House & Museum. While living in Hartford from 1874 to 1891, Twain wrote such works as Adventures of Huckleberry Finn and A Connecticut Yankee in King Arthur's Court. From 1891 on, Twain traveled abroad, wrote, struggled with his own and family illnesses, and lived in New York City. He died at Stormfield, his new home in Redding, Connecticut."

https://connecticuthistory.org/people/samuel-clemens-1835-1910/

[169] "The most traveled of the New York State Bridge Authority's bridges, the Newburgh-Beacon Bridge carries more than 26 million crossings a year on Interstate 84. Preceding construction of the bridge, tradition has it that Native Americans regularly crossed the Hudson River at the point between what is now Beacon and Newburgh, long before Europeans arrived in America."

"Actual bridge construction began in March of 1961. The span was built using riveting to hold the massive steel beams and plates together. Each rivet came from the factory with a cap on one end of the shaft. The red hot rivets would be slid through two pieces of steel by one man. On the other side, another worker with a riveting hammer would pound the scorching metal into a mushroom shape while the rivet was held in place, so there were now two caps on the rivet, with the steel between. As the rivets cooled, they would contract and bring the steel tightly together.

The piers for the bridge were constructed using caissons. They were set into the riverbed and driven down to bedrock using the weight of the caisson while the machines dug out the silt below. The deepest caisson on the Newburgh-Beacon Bridge was set 163 feet below sea level. On November 2, 1963, Governor Nelson Rockefeller cut the gold ribbon on the bridge, opening it to traffic.

Before its construction, it was estimated that the Newburgh-Beacon Bridge would carry 25,000 cars each day, requiring a four-lane design. When funding became difficult, Gov. Rockefeller had decided that the bridge would never carry that many vehicles, and a two-lane structure would be sufficient. Unfortunately by 1964, 25,000 vehicles were using the bridge on a daily basis, and traffic jams were becoming a major problem. The need for greater carrying capacity was critical."

http://www.nysba.state.ny.us/bridgepages/NBB/NBBpage/NYSWeb_nbb_page_NoLogo.htm

[170] "Richmond was founded in 1737 by Colonel William Byrd, II. He inherited the former Stegg lands on both sides of the James River from his father and became known himself as the "Father of Richmond".

He visited Richmond in 1733 and planned to build a city to be called "Richmond". Four years later, his friend, William Mayo made a map of Richmond and the first lots were sold. There were only 250 people living in Richmond when it became a town in 1742. In May of 1782, about two and a half years after the British surrendered at Yorktown, the General Assembly wanted to meet in a central location, less exposed to British incursions than Williamsburg. The first self government was established by the act of incorporation in 1782. Twelve men were to be elected from the City at-large and were to select one of their own to act as Mayor, another to serve as Recorder and four to serve as Aldermen. The remaining six were to serve as members of the Common Council."

http://www.richmondgov.com/CityClerk/documents/CityCouncilList1948_Present_HistorySheet.pdf

[171] "Philip Morris famous spokesperson of over 40 years, Johnny Roventini (1910-1998), began his career as, reportedly, the smallest bellhop ever. Coming in at under 4 feet tall, Roventini resembled a child in stature, later gaining him and Philip Morris popularity among children and adults alike. While working as a bellhop, Roventini was approached by two Philip Morris marketing executives who heard his voice and knew he was an advertising gold mine. They asked for him to call for Philip Morris for one dollar. Johnny, unaware that Philip Morris was a cigarette brand, called out loudly for him. Immediately, the marketing executives saw the promise in Johnny, and enlisted him as the first ever living trademark in their new advertisement campaign. He later appeared on the TV show I Love Lucy alongside stars Lucille Ball and Desi Arnaz, both of whom endorsed Philip Morris in 1959."

http://tobacco.stanford.edu/tobacco_main/images.php?token2=fm_st012.php&token1=fm_img2736.php&theme_file=fm_mt002.php&theme_name=For%20your%20Throat&subtheme_name=Johnny%20Calls%20for%20Philip%20Morris

[172] "The Richmond Braves, a minor league baseball team, played in the New York State League, International Association, Eastern Association, Eastern League and International League between 1966 and 2008."

https://www.statscrew.com/minorbaseball/t-rb14073

[173] "1966 The Triple-A Richmond Braves, an Atlanta Braves farm team, are born. They pick up play in the International League."

"2008 In January, the Atlanta Braves announce their Triple-A franchise would move to Gwinnett County, Ga., after the 2008 season."

https://richmond.com/sports/flying-squirrels/timeline-richmonds-baseball-history/article_c80c864f-8328-55ba-8f14-fd51426b734f.html

[174] "On June 9, Major General Benjamin Butler dispatched about 4,500 cavalry and infantry against the 2,500 Confederate defenders of Petersburg. While Butler's infantry demonstrated against the outer line of entrenchments east of Petersburg, Kautz's cavalry division attempted to enter the city from the south via the Jerusalem Plank Road but was repulsed by Home Guards. Afterwards, Butler withdrew. This was called the battle of old men and young boys by local residents."

http://www.petersburg-va.org/237/Civil-War

[175] "Rocky Mount, city, Nash and Edgecombe counties, east-central North Carolina, U.S., about 50 miles (80 km) east-northeast of Raleigh. The area was settled in the mid-1700s by Virginians after the war (1711–13) with the Tuscarora Indians. The name Rocky Mount, first used in 1816 to designate the location of the area's first post office, was probably derived from the rocky mounds and ridges along its site near the falls of the Tar River. After the arrival of the Wilmington and Weldon Railroad in 1840, it developed as a rail centre and merged with the village of Rocky Mount Hills (established 1818) that had grown around cotton mills by the falls. Rocky Mount was destroyed by Union troops in 1863 during the American Civil War."

https://www.britannica.com/place/Rocky-Mount

[176] "Few places in America have played such a formative role in our country's most defining moments as Fayetteville, from its original settlement in 1739 by Scottish immigrants from the highlands of Scotland arriving via the Cape Fear River, through the deployment of troops to Afghanistan and Iraq today. It is here the very seeds of American freedom, democracy and patriotism were planted and continue to grow.

In 1762, the town of Campbellton, located on the Cape Fear River, was chartered by the colonial assembly. In 1778, Campbellton united with the neighboring town of Cross Creek to become Upper and Lower Campbellton.

In 1783, the North Carolina General Assembly approved the town's official renaming to Fayetteville in honor of the Marquis de Lafayette (1757-1834), the French nobleman who served as a Major General in the Continental Army during the Revolutionary War."

https://www.fayettevillenc.gov/our-city/community/about-fayetteville

[177] "The Sombrero Observation Tower is over 200 feet high and its glass elevator gives riders a full view of South of the Border's grounds as it glides to the top."

https://www.sobpedro.com/attractions

Additional Sources Used in Preparation

US 50

Reader's Digest "The Most Scenic Drives in America", 1997

"US 50 Coast to Coast", Wulf Berg, 1996 http://route50.com/

"Route 66", Michael Karl Witzel, 1996, 2002

https://unusualplaces.org/u-s-route-50-americas-loneliest-road/

https://www.dangerousroads.org/north-america/usa/3755-us-highway-50.html

https://www.santafetrail.org/the-trail/history/history-of-the-sft/

https://route50.com/history.htm

https://roadtripusa.com/the-loneliest-road/

https://www.newsweek.com/2015/06/26/route-50-rode-nowhere-343735.html

US 20

http://historicus20.com/index.html

US 15

"Great American Motorcycle Tours", Gary McKechnie, 2nd Edition, 2002